StoryTime Crafts for Kids

vol. 1

StoryTime Crafts for Kids

vol. 1

Holly Alder

NORTH LIGHT BOOKS
CINCINNATI, OHIO

www.nlbooks.com

No other part of this book may be reproduced in any form or by any electronic or mechanical means including information storage and retrieval systems without permission in writing from the publisher, except by a reviewer, who may quote brief passages in a review. Published by North Light Books, an imprint of F&W Publications, Inc., 1507 Dana Avenue, Cincinnati, Ohio 45207. (800) 289-0963. First edition.

05 04 03 02 01   5 4 3 2 1

Library of Congress Cataloging-in-Publication Data
Alder, Holly.
  Storytime crafts for kids / by Holly Alder.
    p. cm.
  Includes index.
  ISBN 1-58180-059-2 (vol. 1 : alk paper.)
  1. Handicraft. 2. Children's stories. I. Title.
 TT157 .A4195 2000
 745.5—dc21
                        00-027003

Editor: Jane Friedman
Designer: Stephanie Strang
Production coordinator: Emily Gross
Production artist: Kathy Gardner
Photographer: Christine Polomsky and Al Parrish

About the Author

I have greenish eyes that change color without plastic lenses and disappear altogether when I smile, and reddish blonde hair that has been long enough, but never thick enough, to play Lady Godiva. Maybe next time. I have always lived in the Midwest by, and occasionally in, large bodies of water. I presently share a house with two black cats who were born on Halloween and an anorexic Irish setter.

acknowledgments

Thanks

- To the good people at Wilson's Art Store and Jo-Ann Fabrics and Crafts, who supplied most of my materials and answered my "what ifs."

- To Mick, who had to do most of the shopping and pick up the tab.

- To the children who test-drove my ideas and were my sharpest critics.

- And to the wonderful librarians of the Hamilton County Public Library system, who have kept my soul alive.

To my mother and grandmother, who both believed that part of their job here was to make something beautiful.

dedication

Table of

contents

My own introduction to crafts happened shortly after I learned to read. Once my two-years-younger brother started school, my mother filled her empty hours (back when housewives had empty hours) by taking craft classes on weekday afternoons. My mother was very artistic, but impatient with trivial details like instructions, so I was often given the task of reading over the materials the instructor had sent home with her and explaining to my mother how to finish the project—and sometimes finishing the project for her. In the process of becoming skilled at interpreting and simplifying, I often fell in love with the projects myself. I still have a few of the decoupage boxes, beaded flowers, velvet-trimmed cardigans and tin ornaments we made together.

I fell in love with children's books the moment I graduated from Dick and Jane to real picture books. *Green Eyes* by A. Birnbaum was the first picture book I was allowed to check out of the school library—I still remember it. Every year at the school book fair I listed dozens of books I yearned for (even though I knew I would get mostly dolls and clothes for presents), and every summer I told the librarian at our branch of the public library that I was going on vacation, so that I could check out fourteen books at a time instead of the usual two that were allowed. She was nice enough to pretend to believe me, even though I told the same story every two weeks.

When I got to college, both children's books and crafts contributed in equal measure to keeping me sane and connected to a world where gentleness and beauty were still celebrated. I often "paid" myself for the completion of difficult and disagreeable tasks by allowing myself an evening lost in *The Secret Garden* by Frances Hodgson Burnett or an afternoon decorating eggshells begged from the cafeteria.

Then I worked teaching English for twelve years at a small college where the instructors were encouraged to take art classes, if they liked, and to use the studio facilities. There I picked up a love for silk screening and metalsmithing. I have also added stained glass, polymer clay, and bead weaving to my repertoire of nonlucrative skills. I also seem to have added a basement filled with dangerous, nonfeminine tools and nasty, explosive chemicals and an attic so full of boxes of papers, clays, fibers, and beads that insulation has never been a problem.

And all that time I've continued to collect children's books. There was a short period, as my son was growing up, when we had to have two of everything (his copy and my copy), but he turned out to be an artist/musician instead of an artist/reader, and his copies got handed down to nieces and nephews.

Then I took a job managing the children's department of Barnes & Noble Booksellers and was able to settle down to some serious collecting. I presently own over 3,000 of only my very favorite children's books. There's no way I could ever afford to house all the children's books I merely like!

Along with managing the children's department at Barnes & Noble for the past eight years, I've also been in charge of the children's events. Each event featured a book, of course, but since I also loved crafts, I've designed many craft projects over the years to accompany my favorite books. I've tried to develop these crafts with an eye to what the children who showed up for our events would find interesting and fun, but I've also had to accommodate the fact that we were working in the middle of a busy store with both a time limit and a fixed budget.

We had to plan for at least ten participants between the ages of four and ten. We could spend between twenty and thirty dollars. The projects had to be one-shot deals: participants could almost never come back the next week, so we weren't able to do projects that required a lot of drying time. We couldn't get too messy (my worst nightmare was a group that showed up for the store opening to do fingerpainting), and we only had about an hour for each project. Working within these limitations, my goal was for the children to take home an attractive, finished product that they had created by themselves— or with only minimal help.

I allowed two amendments to the "finished" rule. Clays and doughs are too much fun to leave out of any collection of craft projects. Polymer clay objects, therefore, were sent home on a cardboard baking sheet with cooking instructions, and the salt-dough project was sent home with cooking and stringing instructions and the option of painting it or decorating it with crayon designs.

It occurred to me that the parameters I've had to work with have helped me create projects that would be useful for many groups in similar situations. Scout groups, American Girl clubs, commuting art teachers and nursing home activity directors need fun, attractive, successful projects that can be completed in a limited time frame and on a budget, with minimal mess. Thus, the idea for this book was born. Although I have added ideas for further imagining/writing projects for the teacher who will have the students back tomorrow, this is primarily a book for the group leader who needs a quick craft project for a single time slot.

With the on-the-go instructor in mind, I have outlined a shopping list for supplies for each craft for a ten-person group. I've also included a per-participant supplies list to facilitate dividing up the craft materials, preparation instructions, and a step-by-step process for each project. My hope is that you will find these projects irresistible and that you will have a great time making them. It's always wonderful to see how even a four-year-old can move through the steps of an hour-long, multifaceted task for the sake of creating something beautiful.

Supplies: Getting Started

Tools

Tools fall into two categories: those that you will need to have on hand for the participants to use and those that you will need to have at home (or know where to borrow) for preparations. The Basic Tools List covers basic participant tools (for a group of ten) that I like to have on hand all the time because they are used in many different projects.

Basic Tools List
- 10 pairs of scissors
- 10 paper punches
- 10 ballpoint pens
- 10 gluesticks
- 5 bottles of white glue
- 5 staplers
- 5 rulers
- 5 clay blades
- 5 clay rollers
- 3 rolls of clear tape
- 3 rolls of masking tape
- 3 tubes of craft cement
- 10 tapestry needles
- 1 bag of rubber bands
- 1 box of round toothpicks
- 1 box of paperclips
- 1 box of safety pins

Scissors and paper punches

Invest in good scissors: they will have to cut everything from paper to fabric (and sometimes toothpicks). Fabric stores often have sales on brands with both rounded points and really sharp blades. Unfortunately, there doesn't seem to be such a thing as a good paper punch. Expect to replace them frequently—at least they are inexpensive.

Staplers

Office supply stores are also a good source for staplers. I like the handheld squeeze type, which are easier to maneuver, although I occasionally have to help younger children with them because they require a strong grip. It's a good idea to always to have an extra box of staples on hand, too, as you'll often have to reload midproject.

Clay blades

There's no getting around using clay blades if you are making polymer clay objects. They're basically large, single-edged razor blades and must be used with caution. I've never had a child abuse them, but I always give parents the option of sticking around and doing the cutting for younger children. I also only allow five blades on the work table so that I can keep my eye on them. Craft stores are now beginning to carry clay blades, but they're less expensive at local bead stores.

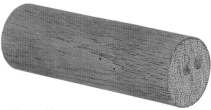

Clay rollers

Craft stores are beginning to carry clay rollers, but it's also easy to make your own. I make mine from pieces left over from old wooden handrails. To make your own, cut a 1½" to 2" wide dowel into 6" lengths (or have your hardware store do this). In a pinch, though, you can use sturdy straight-sided glasses or jars.

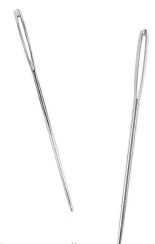

Tapestry needles

Fabric stores carry tapestry needles. I have had no end of trouble with sewing projects—no one can thread a needle anymore—so the only sewing in these projects is done with tapestry needles.

Kitchen tools

Towels, bowls and measuring cups and spoons aren't difficult to assemble (borrow from friends and neighbors if you don't have enough of your own), and the funnel ends of 2 liter bottles can be easily collected after parties.

Miscellaneous tools

Rulers, ballpoint pens, gluesticks, tape, rubber bands and paperclips can be bought at office supply stores in multipacks. I keep an enormous bottle of white glue on hand to fill the children's small bottles. You'll probably have to hit the hardware or craft stores for good craft cement and masking tape. Toothpicks only seem to live at the grocery store, but safety pins are available at both bead shops and fabric stores.

Tools for Preparation

There are also tools that you will need for preparations. These include a small pair of pliers and a small pair of wire cutters for the Silver Snowflakes, a leather punch and hammer for the Leather Bracelets, a compass or awl for the Magic Webs, a large wire cutter and a small handsaw for the Bubble Wands and a good pair of sewing scissors for dividing up felt and fabric. A pair of pinking shears is nice for the fabric ribbons on the Flower Pot Pincushions. If the thought of sawing makes you uncomfortable, you can usually get your local hardware store to do it for you—although it may be expensive.

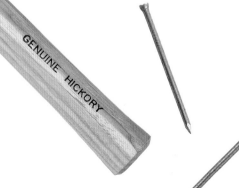

Hardware

You will need ten hammers and ten large nails for the Moon and Stars Lantern project. You will probably have to do some advance work to locate enough people willing to loan theirs (no one that I know has ten—not even me), but this is the only project for which you should expect to have to go hunting.

Materials

Most of the materials you will be using are available at art, craft, fabric, bead, hardware and grocery stores.

Felt

Felt can be bought at most fabric stores in either 9" × 12" (23cm × 31cm) squares or by the yard. Since shopping time is usually limited, I've indicated when you can use either—you never know when the squares or the bolts of the color you need are going to be out of stock. Also, the squares and the bolts go on sale at different times, and my budget necessitated taking advantage of sales. Yardage often comes in both 36" (91cm) and 72" (1.8m) widths. I've given measurements for 36" widths, but if the 72" is on sale, feel free to buy the wider felt. Simply start by cutting it in half widthwise, and then continue with the regular directions.

Yarn and other fibers

The yarn that I use is 4-ply acrylic yarn, which is available at most craft and fabric stores. Embroidery floss is also available for fine work, but I only use the strand whole in these projects. Colored hemp and

string go in and out of fashion, but can usually be found at one craft store or another. The hemp should be black, as the cord elastic (found at fabric stores) used with it to make the Gypsy Anklets doesn't come in natural. In a pinch, thin black string could be substituted.

Leather

Bags of leather scraps are available at craft stores, although if you have a leather shop nearby, you will probably get more of a choice of colors. Make sure that the scraps are long enough to cut out several wrist-size pieces and are sturdy, but not too thick to cut with a good pair of fabric scissors.

Sheet foam

Sheet foam is available at most craft stores. It comes in 9" × 12" (23cm × 31cm) and 12" × 18" (31cm × 46cm) sizes, but the real measurements can vary, so always check and then adjust your patterns if necessary. If you can't get the color you need in the 9" × 12" size, it's okay to buy the 12" × 18" size and cut it in half. Foam also comes in thicknesses (regular, thick and super thick), but for all of the projects in this book, I have used regular (about $\frac{1}{16}$" or 1.6mm).

Paper and cardboard

The handmade paper used for the Folded Paper Birds is available at art stores, as are the small water-color notebooks used for the Col-

lage Covered Scrapbooks. The magazines cut up for the collage itself will have to be scavenged from friends and neighbors. I use tons of cardboard—for patterns, projects and baking sheets. Shirt cardboard still exists, so hit friends who have their laundry professionally done. Cut down thin boxes, save old calendars, whimper at your favorite stores and businesses, and do whatever else you can to build up a large supply without spending money.

Polymer clay

There are many brands of polymer clay. I used Sculpey III for these projects because it is readily available at art and craft stores, is the least expensive, and can be made pliable quickly. The clay should always be kneaded before it is used so that the pieces stick together well. I send the projects home on a piece of cardboard to be baked: at 265°F (129°C) for 20 minutes. The cardboard will not burn at that temperature.

Salt dough

There are many recipes for salt dough. I use two cups (240g) of flour, one cup (288g) of salt, and one scant cup (.2l) of water. This makes enough dough for two participants, so I make it up in three double batches—more than that is too hard to knead by hand. I then divide the dough into individual

12

portions, wrap it in waxed paper, and store it in the refrigerator until craft time. It's best to make the dough the same day you will be using it because it loses its elasticity (gluten) as it sits. I've also found that dough is easier to work with if it's been well chilled. The pieces tend to crack if they are baked at too high a heat, so I bake mine overnight (about eight hours) at 200°F (93°C). However, if you don't feel comfortable with the oven on all night, the pieces can sit out for one night and be baked the next day. They can also be baked in stages if you need to work around meals. They can be baked on a piece of cardboard without worrying about the cardboard burning.

Wire
The 20-gauge wire needed for the Silver Snowflakes can be found at craft stores, but the aluminum clothesline wire needed for the bubble wands is only found at hardware stores.

Wood
The wooden hearts needed for the Love-to-Travel Pins are available at craft stores in assorted sizes. Fabric stores are the best sources for the embroidery hoops used in the Snow and Ice Dreamcatcher and the Space Mobile. The Space

Mobile requires the whole inner hoop of the two-hoop set, but you can use the outer hoop for other projects if you snap off the hardware on the ends and join them back together with masking tape.

Exotic materials
Just about everything else required for these projects is readily available at craft, fabric or hardware stores, but a few things must be acquired from specialty shops. Balloons are best bought from a party supply shop, which will have the greatest variety of colors and sizes in stock. The silver bells needed for the Gypsy Anklets are available at bead shops. The acrylic tubing for the Bubble Wand must be purchased from a plastics manufacturer, but there are usually several in the yellow pages. Pop-top fruit cans will have to be scavenged from neighbors and friends who pack their lunch.

Silver Snowflakes

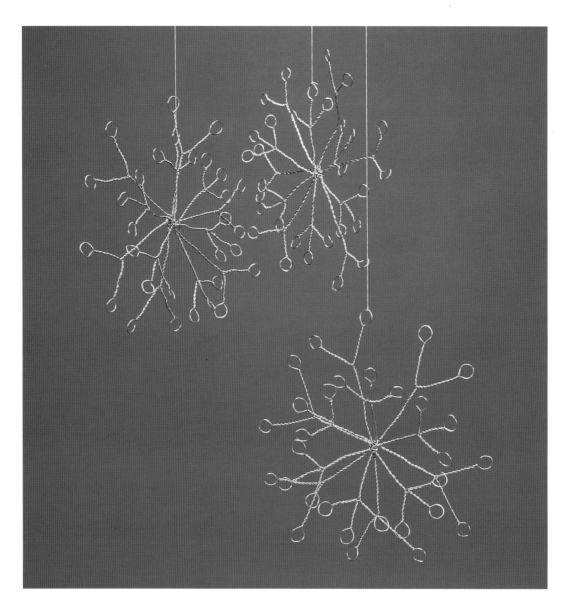

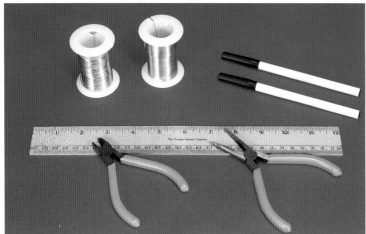

Supplies
• 5 spools of 20-gauge silver wire
• 10 ballpoint pens
• 5 rulers
• small pliers with grips
• wire cutters
Each participant should have two 75" (190.5cm) lengths of wire.

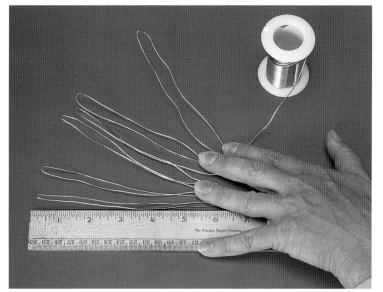

1 Take one wire
and measure
1" (2.5cm) for
the tie-off and
bend it to the
side. Then meas-
ure a loop, 6"
(15cm) up and
6" down. Make
five more loops,
using the first
one as a guide.
Finish by meas-
uring another 1"
(2.5cm) for the
tie-off and bend-
ing it to the
side.

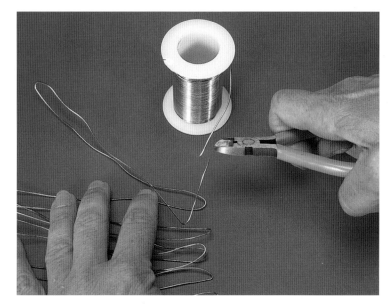

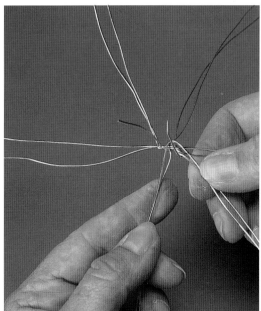

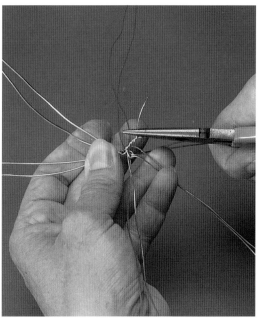

2 Arrange the
loops in a
circle. Poke the
tie-offs through
the center ends
of the loops so
that they are all
fastened togeth-
er in the center
of the circle.
Twist the tie-offs
together firmly
with the pliers.
(**Note:** Younger
children may
need help with
this.)

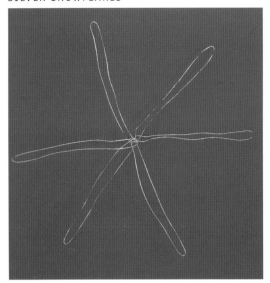

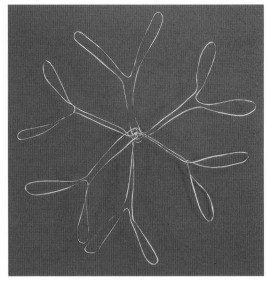

3 Back piece: Bend 2" (5cm) of the outside end of each loop into the middle, forming rabbit ears. Repeat until all six loops have a stem and two ears.

4 Gripping the fork of the ears firmly with your index finger and thumb, twist the stem between the fork and the center of the circle until the two wires are evenly twisted together all the way to the center. Repeat until all six stems are twisted.

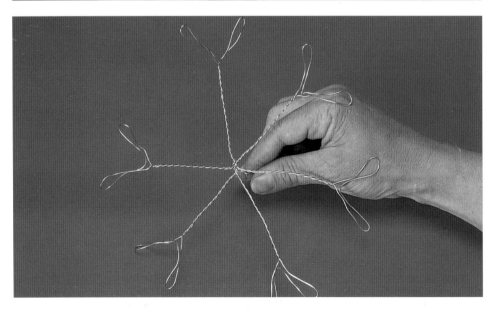

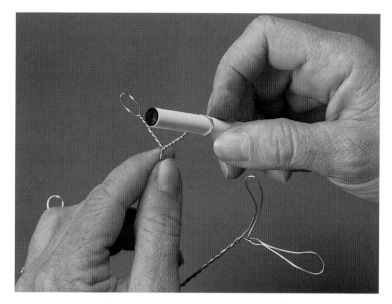

5 Grip the fork of the ears again, making sure the wires meet well down in the fork. Insert a ballpoint pen in the outside end of one of the ears and use it as a twister. Twist until the wires of the ear are evenly twisted from the fork to the ballpoint pen and then remove the pen, leaving a rounded loop at the outside end of the ear. Repeat until all twelve ears are twisted.

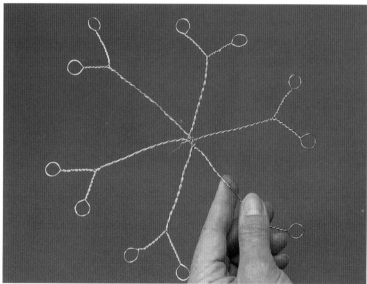

6 Front piece: Repeat steps 1 and 2. Then, instead of forming two rabbit ears, form three by bending each loop in half toward the middle, and then bending the end of the loop back to the outside of the circle, in half again, forming a stem and three rabbit ears. Then do steps 4 and 5.

Featured Book
The Snow Speaks
by Nancy Carlstrom
ill. by Jane Dyer
Little, Brown & Co., 1995

The children know the light, crunchy snow that blows in waves and sprays "as bold as sea salt air." The children hear the snow speaking in scratches and tracks and in sparkling stars and deep winter nights. Are those muffled whispers snow angels, breaking out of the crust to rise, singing?

Related Books
Snowflake Bentley
(Caldecott Honor)
by J. Briggs Martin
ill. by Mary Azarian
Houghton Mifflin, 1998

Millions of Snowflakes
by Mary McKenna Siddals
ill. by Elizabeth Sayles
Houghton Mifflin, 1998

Imagining/Writing
The African child said, "I have never seen snow. Tell me about it. I have heard that it is very beautiful and very dangerous, that it is very small but it can fill a whole valley. How can this be?"

Assembly: Lay the front piece on top of the back piece, poking the tie-off from the front piece through the center of the back piece. Twist both tie-offs together, cut off all but ¼" (6mm), and bend the end back toward the center. Arrange your snowflake so that all of the stems and ears are fairly evenly spaced. Remember, no two snowflakes are supposed to look the same, and each one is always perfect. Also, if your time is limited, just make the front piece.

Dragon Helmets

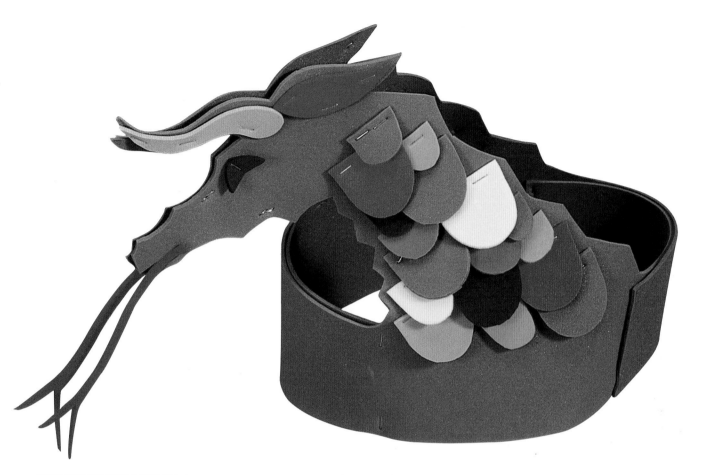

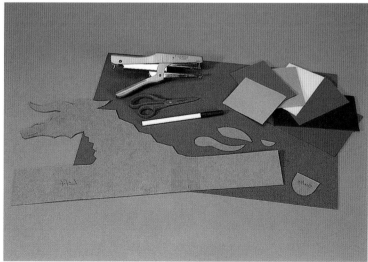

Preparation

Transfer the dragon helmet pattern from page 115 onto cardboard. Cut three patterns and tape the sections together. Also trace patterns for eyes, horns and ears onto cardboard. Cut three of each. (Scales and tongues are cut freehand.) Cut red foam into 1" × 9" (2.5cm × 23cm) strips. Cut the rest of the 9" × 12" (23cm × 31cm) sheets into quarters and then thirds, to make 3" × 3" (8cm × 8cm) pieces.

1 Place the bottom of the cardboard dragon helmet pattern on one of the long sides of the foam. Trace around it. Turn the pattern around and place it on the other long side of the fun foam. Trace around it again. Cut out the two dragon helmet pieces.

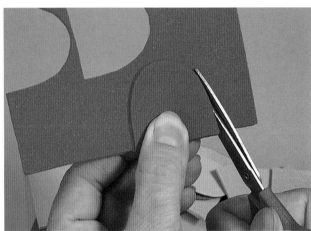

2 While waiting to use the dragon pattern, cut scales from the assorted foam colors. Trace around the eye, horn and ear patterns, using black for the eye, gray for the horn and red for the ear. Cut two of each. Cut two letter *Y*s about 4" (10cm) long and as thin as possible out of red for the tongues.

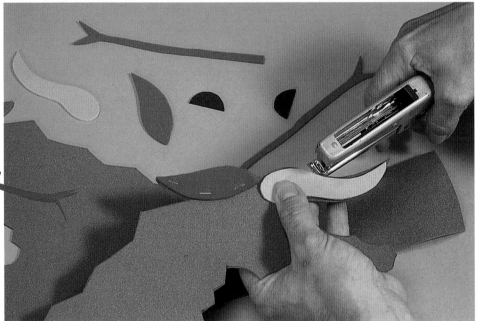

3 Using a stapler, attach an ear, a horn and a tongue to each side of the helmet.

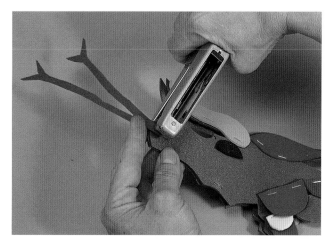

4 Starting from the bottom of the neck, attach rows of scales to the dragon helmet with the flat edge on top and angled toward the ear. Put one or two staples across the top of each scale. Vary the colors and sizes of scales in each row. Overlap each row so that as few of the staples show as possible. Stop about ½″ (13mm) from the ear.

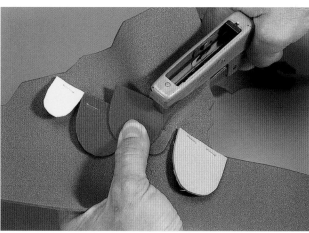

5 Put the "wrong" sides of the dragon helmet together. Staple the head of the dragon in three places: beside the eye, at the bottom of the cheek and through the tongues. Staple from each side for extra strength. Using paperclips, overlap the front and back bands of the helmet, adjusting them to fit your head. Staple together at each end, top and bottom, front and back. Staple from both sides for extra strength. Remove paperclips.

Featured Book
Raising Dragons
by Jerdine Nolen
ill. by Elise Primavera
Harcourt Brace & Co., 1998

Ma and Pa weren't too keen on the idea of their daughter raising a dragon, but the dragon turned out to be really useful on the farm—plowing the fields, tending the crops and keeping all the varmints away. And even when the dragon accidentally torched a field of corn, the family was able to sell the dragon-popped corn for a tidy sum. Best popcorn anybody had ever tasted!

Related Books
Komodo!
by Peter Sis
ill. by Peter Sis
Morrow, William & Co., 1999

Dragon
by Wayne Anderson
ill. by Wayne Anderson
Simon & Schuster, 1992

Imagining/Writing
When you answered the door this morning, you found a small dragon sitting on your doorstep. A note was attached to her collar: "Called to the country for the weekend. Please take care of Sparks."

Leather Bracelets

Supplies
- 2 half-pound (.23kg) bags of suede or leather scraps
- 7 yards (6.4m) of black leather cord
- 80 assorted-color pony beads
- 1 package of felt tip pens
- animal rubber stamps and stamp pad (optional)
- fabric shears or rotary blade and mat
- leather punch
- hammer
- scrap paper
- cardboard

To make two bracelets, each participant should have two 6" × 1¼" (15cm × 3cm) leather strips, two 12" (31cm) lengths of leather cords and eight pony beads.

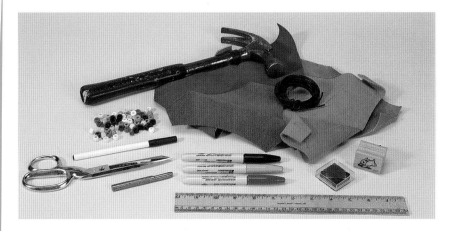

1 Punch two holes, evenly spaced and not too near the edges, in each end of the leather strip. (Take turns doing this while the others are planning their designs.)

Preparation
Cut twenty 6"× 1¼" (15cm× 3cm) strips from the leather scraps with fabric shears or a rotary blade. Cut the leather cord into 12" (31cm) pieces.

2 Thread a piece of leather cord up through one end of the strip, across the top and down through the other end.

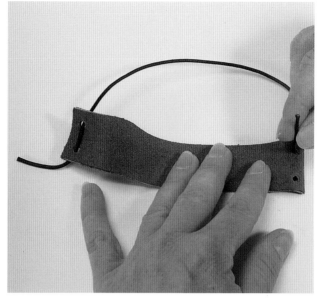

3 Thread two pony beads on each cord end. Tie an overhand knot below the pony beads at the end of each cord.

4 Decorate the front of the leather strip with magic markers and rubber stamps. Tie the bracelet on with an overhand knot. (You may need a friend to help with this.)

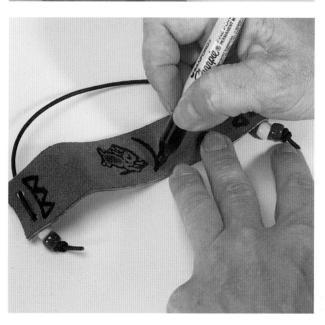

Featured Book
The Rough-Face Girl
by Rafe Martin
ill. by David Shannon
Putnam Publishing, 1998

On the shore of Lake Ontario stood a huge wig-wam where it was said that a great, rich, powerful and handsome Invisible Being lived. But only the woman who could truly see him could become his wife. Many women had tried—wealthy, beautiful women. So how could the poor, ugly Rough-Face Girl, who tend-ed ashes, think she had a chance?

Related Books
Moonstick: The Seasons of the Sioux
by Eve Bunting
ill. by John Sandford and Joanna Colter
HarperCollins, 2000

Frog Girl
by Paul Owen Lewis
ill. by Paul Owen Lewis
Tricycle Press, 1999

Imagining/Writing
The design on your bracelet is a magic symbol. When you touch it with the first two fingers of your left hand, close your eyes, and whisper "Come out," your animal totem will appear. What kind of animal has chosen to be your totem?

Soft Felt Boxes

Supplies
- 3 colors of felt, either 1 yard (91cm) of each color (36" wide yardage) or 8 pieces of 9" × 12" felt (23cm × 31cm) of each color (24 total)
- 10 hanks of variegated embroidery thread
- 10 pairs of scissors
- 10 ballpoint pens
- 5 staplers
- 10 tapestry needles
- mat knife
- cardboard

Each participant should have two 9" × 12" (23cm × 31cm) pieces of felt, shared felt scraps and one hank of variegated embroidery thread.

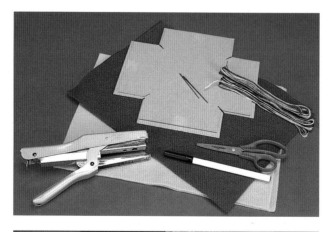

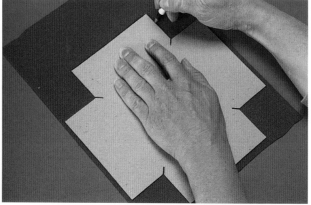

Preparation
Trace patterns on page 116 for box top and bottom onto cardboard. Cut three sets. Use a mat knife to cut clips into each corner. Mark "top" and "bottom," as they are easily confused. Also, cut five 4" × 4" (10cm × 10cm) cardboard squares for wrapping tassels. If felt is yardage, fold in quarters, then thirds, and cut twelve 9" × 12" (23cm × 31cm) pieces.

1 Choose two squares each, and pass the patterns around until each person has traced a top and a bottom. Cut out just inside the pen lines. Don't forget to clip ¼" (6mm) into each corner.

2 Fold the box top so that the two edges of the first corner are lined up together.

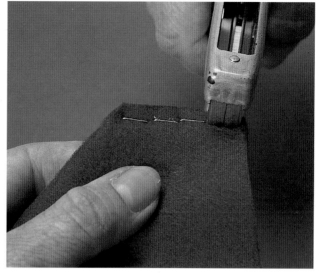

3 Staple ¼″ (6mm) in from the edge, using three or four staples in a straight, even line.

4 Refold, and then repeat the process for the three other corners. Fold and staple the corners of the box bottom in the same manner.

5 Turn the stapled corners to the inside.

6 Choose a hank of embroidery thread. Before wrapping it around the cardboard, cut two double-fold lengths (about 12″ or 31cm each) off of it and set them aside. Then wrap the remaining thread around the 4″ (10cm) piece of cardboard as many times as it will go to make a tassel. Cut through the bottom of the tassel.

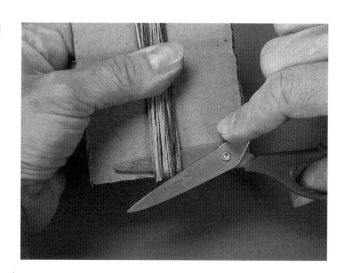

7 Tie the top loop of the tassel together with one of the reserved lengths, using a double overhand knot.

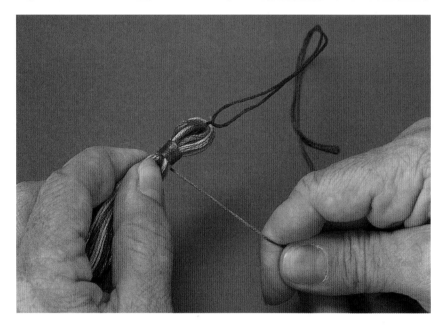

8 Using the other reserved length of thread, wrap the tassel, starting about ½" (13mm) from the top, for about ½". Tie it with a double overhand knot, smooth the extra threads into the tassel and trim.

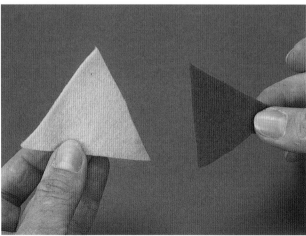

9 Exchange the different colored felt scraps, and cut decorative shapes for the box top.

10 Thread one of the ties left at the top of the tassel through a tapestry needle. Center your decorative shapes on the box top and then poke the needle through the center of the stack and through the box top.

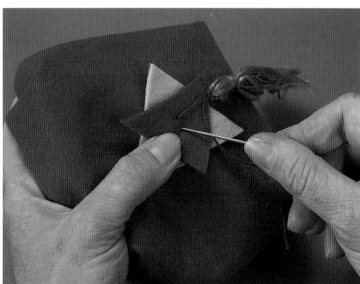

11 Repeat with the other tie, but poke down through the stack about ⅛" (3mm) from the first hole.

12 Tie the threads under the box top with a double overhand knot, then cut off to about 1/4" (6mm).

Frog Bookmarks

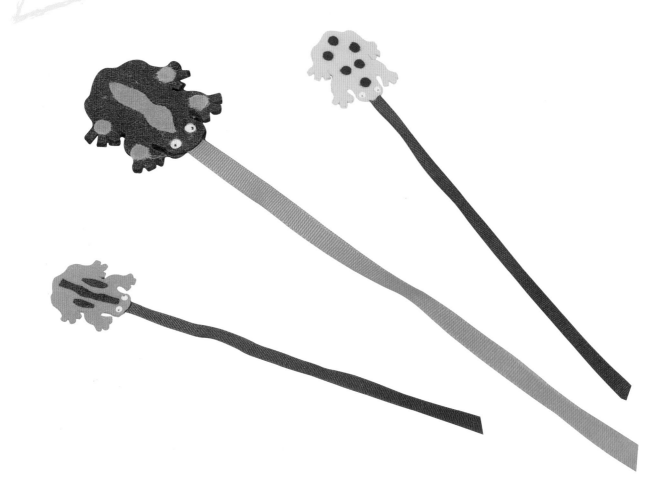

Supplies
- ten 9" × 12" (23cm × 31cm) felt squares (or scraps) in exotic frog colors: blue, green, yellow, red and orange
- 10 yards of ¼" (6mm) grosgrain ribbon in the same colors
- sixty ⅛" (3mm) glue-on googly eyes
- 10 pairs of scissors
- 10 ballpoint pens
- 5 staplers
- 5 bottles of white glue
- 10 paper punches
- cardboard

To make three bookmarks, each participant should have three felt square thirds (or scraps), three 12" (31cm) lengths of ribbon and six googly eyes.

1 For each frog,
trace pattern
onto felt twice
and cut out,
cutting just in-
side the pen
lines.

2 Choose a rib-
bon of a con-
trasting color.
Center one end
of the ribbon
over the bottom
felt frog piece.
Staple the ribbon
to the felt in
four places.

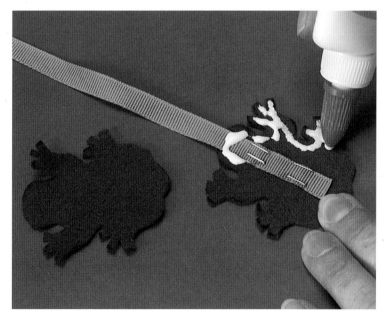

3 Glue the top felt frog piece over the stapled ribbon. Be sure to
spread the glue all the way to the toes.

Featured Book
Red-Eyed Tree Frog
by Joy Cowley
photos by Nic Bishop
Scholastic Inc., 1999

The red-eyed tree frog sleeps all day, but at night he wakes up hungry. What can he find to eat? Can he jump fast enough and far enough to stay out of the way of other hungry creatures who would like to eat him?

Related Books
Tuesday
(Caldecott Honor)
by David Wiesner
ill. by David Wiesner
Houghton Mifflin Co., 1997

Bullfrog Pops!
by Rick Walton
ill. by Chris McAllister
Gibbs Smith, 1999

Imagining/Writing
You have decided to train a frog for the state fair frog jumping competition. Where will you catch your frog? How will you train him? How far will he have to jump to win?

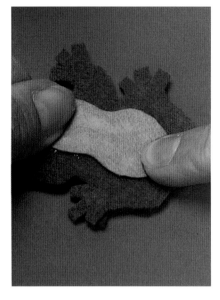

4 Cut strips of felt the same color as your ribbon and glue them to the frog's tummy, using some of them to cover the staples.

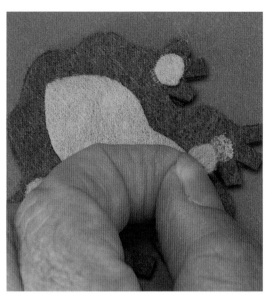

5 Make small felt dots with the paper punch and glue them on.

6 Turn the frog right side up and glue on two googly eyes. Decorate the frog's back with more dots and stripes.

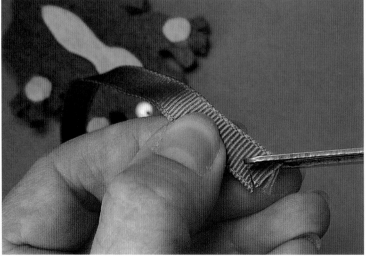

7 Cut a notch in the end of your ribbon.

Juggling Apples
and Pumpkins

Supplies
- sixty 12" (31cm) round balloons:
  30 orange and 30 red
- 60 green satin or velvet leaves
  on wire stems
- 20 lbs. (9kg) flour (60 cups
  needed; 5 lb. bag = 17 cups)
- ten 2-liter bottles
- 10 ballpoint pens or pencils
- 10 permanent black pens
- several bowls
- several large spoons or cups
- utility scissors

Each participant should have three
red balloons, three orange balloons,
six leaves and shared flour.

Preparation
Empty the flour into large bowls. Cut 2-liter bottles in half. (Save bases to use as bowls for other projects.)

1 Pull the neck of the balloon over the funnel end of a 2-liter bottle and hold it firmly. Scoop flour into the funnel, about ¼ cup (31g) at a time. Using the back end of the pen or pencil, tamp the flour down into the balloon. The balloon should expand to take about 1 cup (125g) of flour.

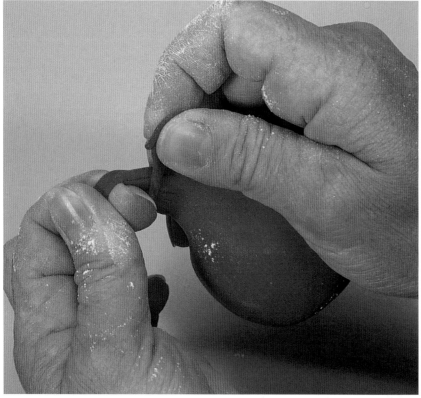

2 Tie the balloon off at the top with an overhand knot. Repeat until each participant has filled six balloons: three red and three orange.

3 Select a leaf and wrap the wire around the tied-off end of each balloon, beneath the knot.

4 If you like, draw a smiling face on the apples and a jack-o'-lantern face on the pumpkins with permanent markers. Let dry.

Featured Book
Apples and Pumpkins
by Anne Rockwell
ill. by Lizzy Rockwell
Simon & Schuster, 1989

When the leaves turn red and yellow, the Comstock Farm is the place to go to pick apples and pumpkins. Geese, chickens and a big, fat turkey walk with us to the apple trees and watch while we fill our bushel baskets. Then they help us choose the right pumpkin for a scary jack-o'-lantern.

Related Books
Pumpkin Soup
by Helen Cooper
ill. by Helen Cooper
Farrar, Straus & Giroux, 1999

Rain Makes Applesauce
(Caldecott Honor)
by Julian Scheer
ill. by Marvin Bileck
Holiday House Inc., 1976

Imagining/Writing
Farmer's Orchard is having a contest. They are awarding a grand prize for the best new dish made out of apples or pumpkins. What dish will you enter in the contest? What are the other contestants making? And what does the grand prize turn out to be?

Sock Snowmen

Supplies
- 10 white ankle-length socks
- two 12-oz. (340g) bags of polyester stuffing
- twenty ½" (13mm) googly eyes
- 30 black mini pompoms
- 20 rubber bands
- six 3½–4 oz. (100g) skeins of acrylic yarn: 2 red, 2 white, 2 green
- 10 pairs of scissors
- 5 bottles of white glue
- cardboard

Each participant should have one white sock, two googly eyes, three mini pom-poms, two rubber bands and shared stuffing and yarn.

Preparation
Cut five 12" × 2"
(31cm × 5cm)
pieces of
cardboard.

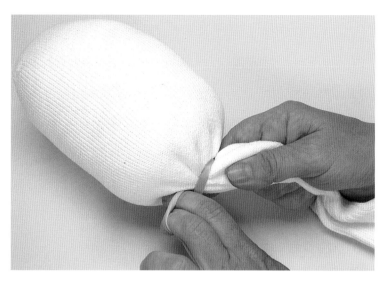

1 Stuff bottom half of the sock firmly with poly-ester stuffing. Tie off with a rubber band.

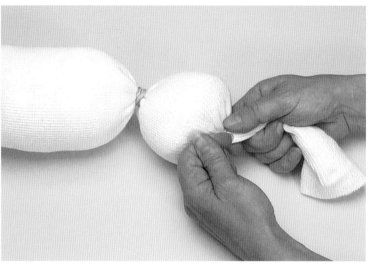

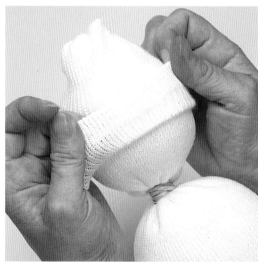

2 Divide remaining half in half again, stuff firmly with stuffing and tie off with a rubber band.

3 Pull cuff halfway down over the snowman's head to look like a ribbed cap. Turn up rim.

4 Wrap red yarn thirty times around the 2" (5cm) side of the cardboard.

5 Cut threads on both ends, keeping them together in a neat stack.

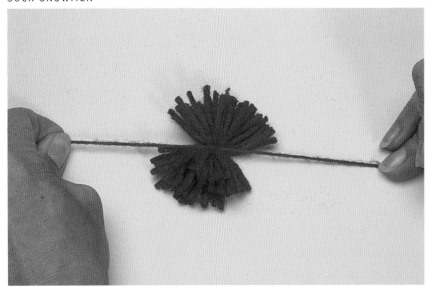

6 Cut a piece of yarn about 6″ (15cm) long, and tie it around the stack tightly with two overhand knots. Trim the ends to the width of the pom-pom. Set aside.

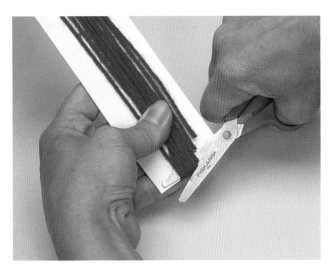

7 Wrap red yarn around the 12″ (31cm) side of the cardboard 12 times. Cut threads only on bottom end and open threads out to 24″ (61cm).

8 Repeat with white yarn and green yarn. Pile all three colors together and tie one end with an overhand knot, leaving a 1″ (2.5cm) tassel.

9 Separate colors and braid to within 2″ (5cm) of the end. Tie off with an overhand knot.

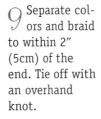

10 Trim tassel to 1" (2.5cm). Wrap scarf around the snowman's neck and tie loosely.

11 Glue red pom-pom to top of hat.

12 Glue black mini pom-pom buttons to the snowman's tummy. Cut a smile of red yarn, and then glue the smile and googly eyes to face.

Featured Book
The Biggest, Best Snowman
by Margery Cuyler
ill. by Will Hillenbrand
Scholastic Inc., 1998

Little Nell is always too little. Her big mother and big sisters won't let her help out with anything at home. But her forest friends, Reindeer, Hare and Bear Cub, want Nell to show them how to make a snowman. Can she make the biggest, best snowman that ever was?

Related Books
The Snowman
by Raymond Briggs
ill. by Maggie Downer
Random House, 1999

The Snowchild
by Debi Gliori
ill. by Debi Gliori
Simon & Schuster, 1998

Imagining/Writing
You want to build the biggest snowman in the world. You talk to your friends about your idea. They all want to help, but they have some unusual ideas. What will you use to support the snowman? How big will it be? How long will it take to build?

Puffy Felt Stars

Supplies

- light gray and tan felt: one yard (91cm) each of 36″ (91cm) felt or ten 9″ × 12″ (23cm × 31cm) felt squares (20 total)
- ½ yard (46cm) of 60″ (1.5m) polyester batting
- 4 yards (3.6m) of gold cord
- 3 squeeze bottles each of gold and silver glitter glue
- cardboard
- 10 pairs of scissors
- 10 ballpoint pens
- 5 staplers
- safety pins

Each participant should have one 9″ × 12″ (23cm × 31cm) piece of grey felt, one 9″ × 12″ piece of tan felt, one 6″ × 10″ (15cm × 25cm) piece of batting, one 12″ (31cm) piece of gold cord and one piece of cardboard.

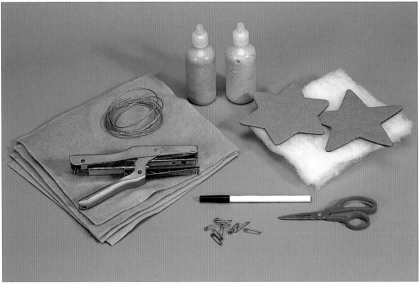

Preparation

Transfer the 5-point and 6-point star patterns from page 117 onto cardboard. Cut three of each. If felt is yardage, fold it in quarters and then in thirds, and cut twelve 9" × 12" (23cm × 31cm) pieces. Fold the batting in half widthwise, in half lengthwise, then in thirds lengthwise, and cut into twelve 6" × 10" (15cm × 25cm) pieces. Cut the gold cord into 12" (31cm) pieces.

1 Draw around either the 5-point or 6-point star pattern twice on the grey felt. Cut out just inside the pen lines. Repeat with the tan felt.

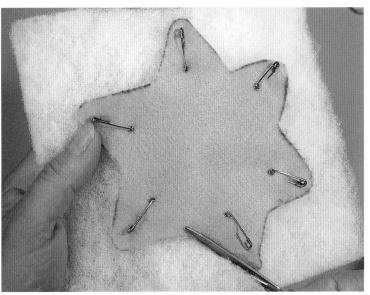

2 Pin one of each color felt star to the batting, using one safety pin in each point. Cut batting to the size of the star, being careful not to cut the felt. Unpin the felt stars and trim ¼" (6mm) from all sides of the batting stars.

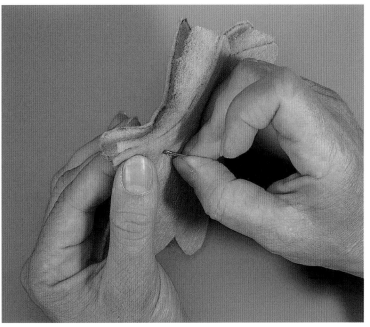

3 Center one of the batting stars between the gray felt stars. Center the other batting star between the tan felt stars. Pin together with safety pins, leaving one point unpinned.

Featured Book

Nora's Stars
by Satomi Ichikawa
ill. by Satomi Ichikawa
Putnam Publishing, 1997

Nora wants the stars to come and play. They look beautiful, shimmering and glimmering on her bedspread, and they fit just fine into her toy box. But the sky looks dark and sad without any stars. Maybe the stars really belong in the sky after all.

Related Books

Draw Me a Star
by Eric Carle
ill. by Eric Carle
Putman Publishing, 1992

Twinkle, Twinkle Little Star
by Jane Taylor
ill. by Julia Noonan
Scholastic, Inc., 1992

Imagining/Writing

One morning when you walk to school, you see a star lying on the sidewalk. You figure it must have fallen out of the sky, but you don't know how to put it back. So you put it in your pocket and take it with you. Who can you ask for advice?

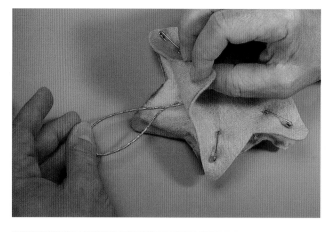

4 Cut gold cord in half and tie ends of each piece with an overhand knot. Place the knot at the center of the batting so the loop hangs out of one of the points of the star. Safety pin the final point.

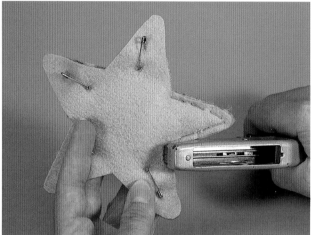

5 Staple along each edge of the star-and-batting sandwich, making a neat row of staples ¼" (6mm) from the edge. Be sure that the staples secure the gold cord loop on each side of the point.

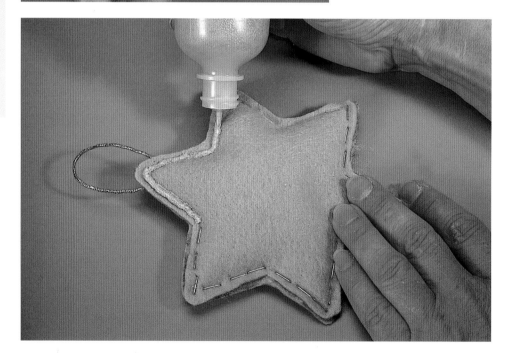

6 Carefully squeeze a line of glitter along the row of staples on the top side of the star. Wait a few minutes to let the glue set. With only your thumb and finger in the middle of the star, turn it over and carefully squeeze a line of glitter along the row of staples on the bottom side of the star. Repeat steps four through six for second star. Carry stars home on a piece of cardboard. Let dry thoroughly before hanging.

Magic Webs

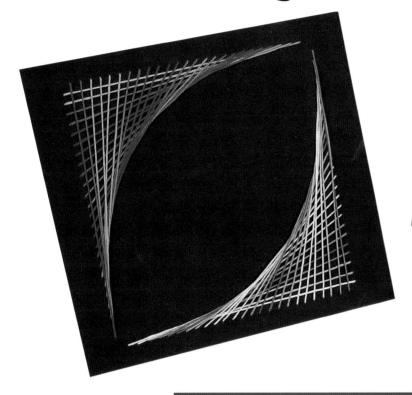

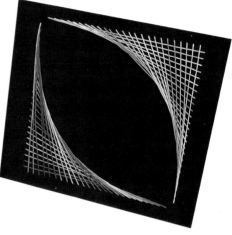

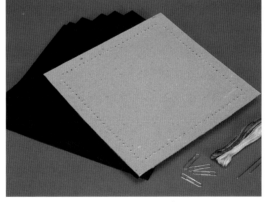

Supplies
- 20 hanks of variegated embroidery thread
- ten 9″ × 12″ (23cm × 31cm) sheets of black foam
- 10 paperclips
- 10 tapestry needles
- 5 pairs of scissors
- 1 roll of clear tape
- compass or awl
- five rulers
- cardboard

Each participant should have two hanks of embroidery thread and one sheet of 9″ × 9″ (23cm × 23cm) black foam.

Preparation

Cut a 9″ (23cm) square of cardboard. Measure in ⅝″ (16mm) on each side and draw a line. Mark every ¼″ (6mm) on each of the four sides. Using the point of a compass, pierce through every mark, except the four corners of the square. Cut the sheets of foam into 9″ (23cm) squares. Center the cardboard pattern over the foam. Pierce through the cardboard pattern to create the same pattern of holes in each sheet of foam.

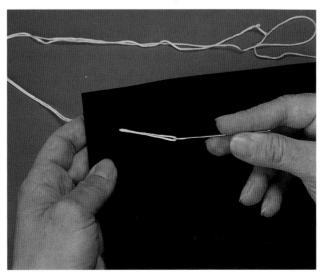

1 Choose two hanks of embroidery thread in contrasting colors. Cut a piece about 2′ (61cm) long from the first color. Tie a double overhand knot in one end of the thread, and thread the other end through a tapestry needle. Starting at the upper left-hand corner of the top row of holes, bring the thread up through the first hole.

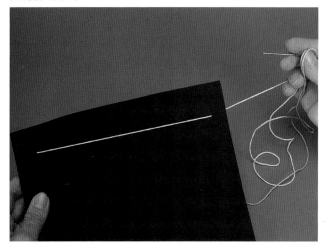 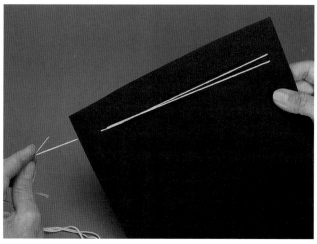

2 Thread down through the top hole in the row of holes on the right side. Come up through the second hole on the right side, and back down through the second hole on the top. Proceed from left to right across the top, and from top to bottom down the right side, drawing most of your thread across the front of the square and leaving only ¼" (6mm) stitches on the back.

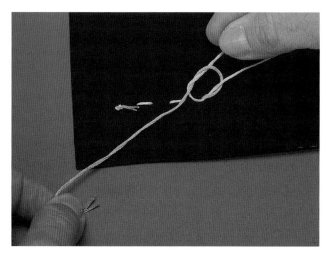

3 When your thread is too short to go across the front again, cut another piece and tie it on in the back with two overhand knots. Trim the ends of the thread to ¼" (6mm). When you have completed the first two sides of the square, tie the thread close to the back with a double overhand knot and trim.

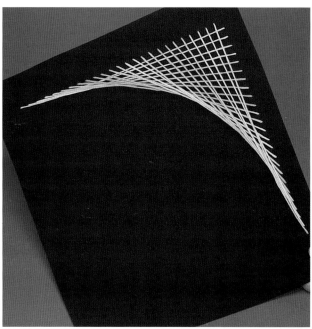

Featured Book
Miss Spider's Tea Party
ill. by David Kirk
Scholastic Inc., 1994

Miss Spider wants to invite all of the other insects for tea at her web, but they're all afraid that they will be the main course. How can Miss Spider convince them that she only wants to be friends (and that she's really a vegetarian!)?

Related Books
Space Spinners
by Suse MacDonald
ill. by Suse MacDonald
Penguin USA, 1991

The Very Busy Spider
by Eric Carle
ill. by Eric Carle
Putnam Publishing, 1995

Imagining/Writing
Your science experiment has gotten way out of hand. You were trying to breed a spider that would go after flies instead of just waiting for them to come to her, but your spider is as big as a baseball now, and she's spinning around your room so fast you had to dive behind the bed to keep from being webbed. What will you do now?

4 Cut a thread of your second color, knot it, and thread it through the needle. This time, come up through the first hole in the lower right corner of the bottom row of holes, and come back down in the bottom hole of the row of holes on the left side. Proceed from right to left across the bottom, and from bottom to top up the left side, again drawing most of your thread across the front of the square. Rethread when necessary.

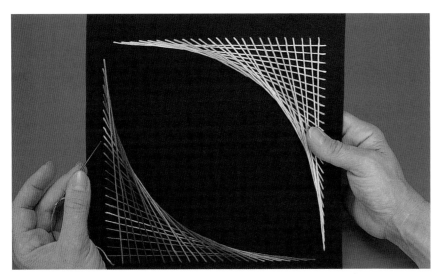

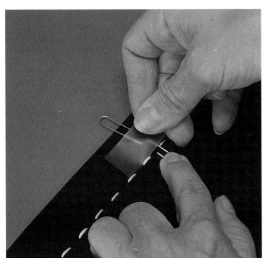

5 When you have completed the last two sides of the square, tie the thread close to the back with a double overhand knot. Unbend a paper clip and center it behind the top row of stitching. Secure with two pieces of clear tape. Hang it up and enjoy.

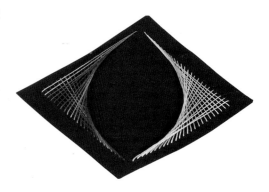

Love to Travel Pins

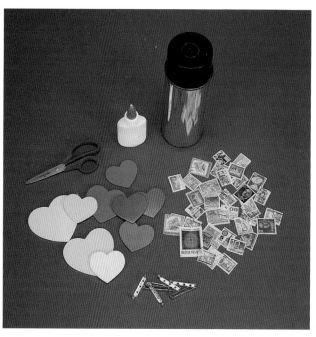

Supplies
- approximately 50 pre-cut wooden heart shapes (assorted sizes, painted or plain)
- 200 world stamps
- twnety 1½" (4cm) pin backings
- 10 pairs of scissors
- 5 bottles of white glue
- spray can of clear instant shoe polish
- newspaper

To make two pins, each participant should have five hearts, twenty stamps, and two pin backings.

1 Choose two or three heart shapes for each pin. Choose stamps of similar themes or colors and arrange them on hearts in overlapping patterns. Glue in place (use glue sparingly so the stamps don't pucker).

2 When stamps overlap the edges of the hearts, trim them with scissors.

3 Glue smaller shapes on top of larger ones, off-center and slightly overlapping.

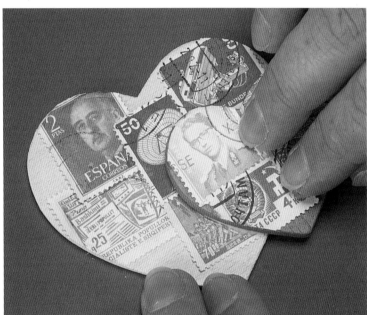

4 Glue a pin backing on the back of the largest heart. Place it about ½" (13mm) higher than the center of the heart so the pin won't tip forward when you wear it.

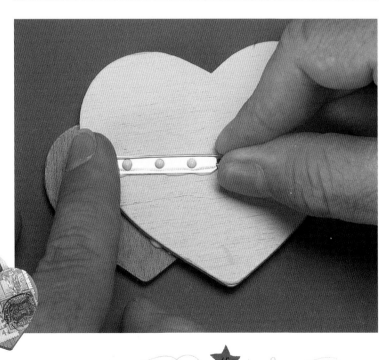

Featured Book
Someplace Else
(Reading Rainbow)
by Carol Saul
ill. by Barry Root
Simon & Schuster, 1997

All her life Mrs. Tillby had lived in the white house by the apple orchard, but all her life she had wondered what it would be like to live someplace else. First she visits the city, then the seashore, then the mountains, a cabin by a lake, a fire tower above a forest, an adobe hut in the desert and a riverboat. She always says that if the place suits her, she'll stay, but she's always longing to see someplace else. Then she finds the perfect solution!

Related Books
How to Make an Apple Pie and See the World
by Marjorie Priceman
ill. by Marjorie Priceman
Random House, 1996

Toot and Puddle
by Holly Hobbie
ill. by Holly Hobbie
Little, Brown & Co., 1997

Imagining/Writing
You have won a trip to the most interesting place in the world, everything is paid for and you are allowed to bring your best friend. But you must agree to deliver a yellow envelope to the Count of Nevereturn Castle in the Forbidden Forest.

Final Touch
After the pins are completed, place them on sheets of newspaper, and spray the fronts with a coat of clear instant shoe polish to protect the stamps. Let them dry a few minutes before handling.

Collage Scrapbooks

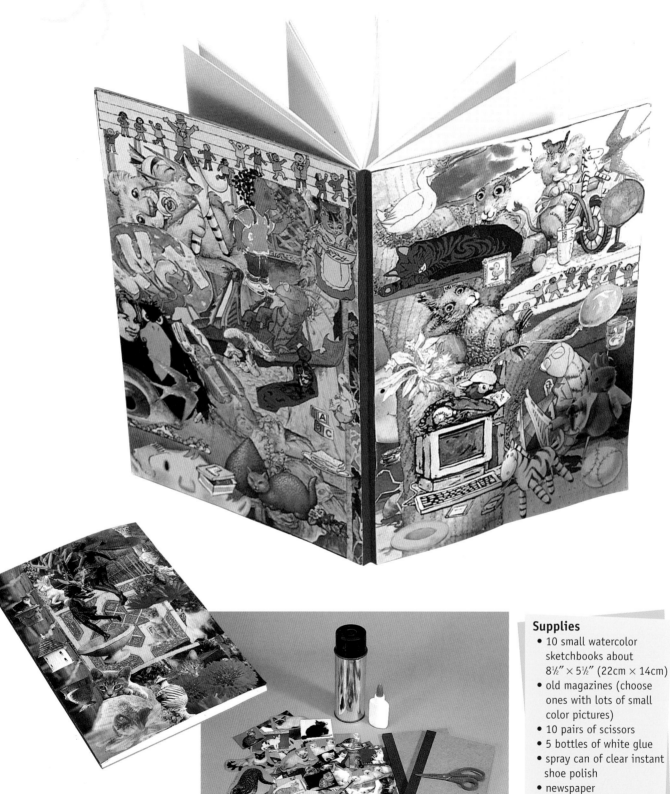

Supplies
- 10 small watercolor sketchbooks about 8½″ × 5½″ (22cm × 14cm)
- old magazines (choose ones with lots of small color pictures)
- 10 pairs of scissors
- 5 bottles of white glue
- spray can of clear instant shoe polish
- newspaper

Each participant should have one sketchbook and shared magazines.

1 Cut out two or three large pictures to fill in the background. Overlap them to cover the whole front of the scrapbook. Glue them down, using the glue sparingly so that the pictures don't pucker. With scissors, trim off any excess even with the edges of the cover. Repeat with the back of the sketchbook.

Featured Book
Amelia's Notebook
by Marissa Moss
ill. by Marissa Moss
Pleasant Co., 1999

Have you ever kept a diary or a journal, or made a scrapbook? Amelia starts to record her life when she's about to move to a new house and a new school and she's absolutely miserable. Mom says that writing in her notebook will help make her feel better, but Amelia isn't sure that it can.

Related Books
Carl Makes a Scrapbook
by Alexandra Day
ill. by Alexandra Day
Farrar, Strauss & Giroux, 1994

Simon's Book
(Reading Rainbow)
by Henrik Drescher
ill. by Henrik Drescher
Morrow, William & Co., 1991

2 Cut medium-size pictures to fill in the middle ground. Place them over the seams in the background pictures. Cut around all the details only on the parts that aren't going to be covered up. Glue down and then trim the edges if necessary.

Imagining/Writing
You have a time capsule, and in it you are going to put a scrapbook that will show your grandchildren all the things you long to do and see. What kinds of pictures will you need?

3 Cut small pictures to fill in the foreground. Cut around all the details, but continue to overlap the pictures to hide seams and create a dimensional look.

Final Touch
Place scrapbooks on sheets of old newspaper and spray with instant shoe polish to protect the pictures. Let dry a few minutes. Take home and fill the scrapbook with your mementos and treasures.

Drowsy Mice

Supplies
- five 3½–4 oz. (100g) skeins of gray acrylic yarn
- three 9" × 12" (23cm × 31cm) gray felt squares
- 20 ½" (13mm) sew-on googly eyes
- 10 black mini pom-poms
- 10' (3m) of black plastic lacing
- 10 pairs of scissors
- 10 ballpoint pens
- 5 bottles of white glue
- 10 tapestry needles
- cardboard

Each participant should have one quarter of a gray felt square, one black mini pom-pom, two googly eyes, 12" (31cm) black lacing and shared gray yarn.

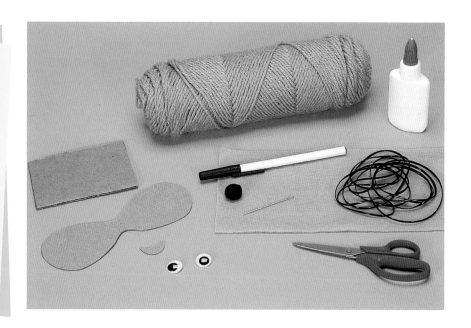

Cut ten 4″ × 3″ (10cm × 8cm) cardboard rectangles. Trace patterns from page 124 for ears and eyebrows and cut three of each. Divide felt squares into twelve 3″ × 9″ (8cm × 23cm) pieces.

1 Share yarn with a partner, one pulling from the inside of the skein and one from the outside. Wind the yarn around the 4″ (10cm) side of the cardboard forty times. Cut through the yarn on both ends. Repeat and lay the second winding down in a separate pile.

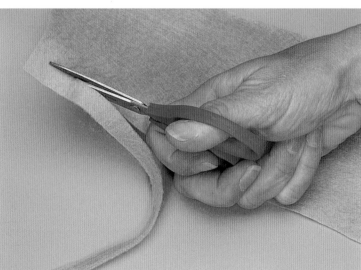

2 Cut a thin 9″ (23cm) long tail off of the 9″ edge of your felt. Taper it to a point.

3 Lay the square end of the tail down on the bottom pile of windings, overlapping the middle by ½″ (13mm). Lay the other pile of windings on top of the bottom pile and the tail.

4 Cut a piece of yarn about 6″ (15cm) long, and tie the pile into a tight ball.

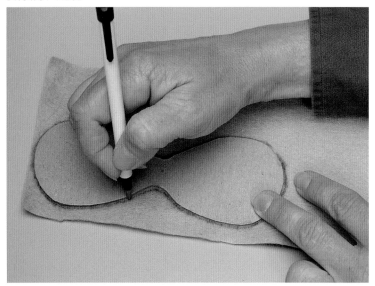

5 Trace around the ear pattern and cut it out, cutting just inside the pen lines.

6 Repeat step 1, except wind the yarn around the 3" (8cm) side of the cardboard thirty times. Cut through the yarn on both ends. Repeat, and lay the second winding down in a separate pile. Lay the ears down across the bottom pile of 3" (8cm) windings and lay the top pile of windings over it. Cut a piece of yarn about 6" (15cm) long and tie the pile into a tight ball.

7 Use the tying strings from the larger ball to tie it to the smaller ball, behind the ears, with a double overhand knot. Make sure the ties from the small ball are in the center of the face.

8 Trim the tied ends even with the windings.

9 Thread one end of the ties from the small ball onto a tapestry needle. Thread on one googly eye.

10 Thread the other end of the ties onto the needle. Thread on a second googly eye. Tie both ends of the ties tightly between the eyes with a double overhand knot.

11 Cut three 4" (10cm) pieces of plastic lacing.

12 Center the whiskers on the face, and tie under the eyes with a double overhand knot. Trim the yarn ends close to the knot.

Featured Book
You Silly Goose
by Ellen Stoll Walsh
ill. by Ellen Stoll Walsh
Harcourt Brace & Co., 1996

George the mouse and
Emily the goose were very
good friends. When George
sees a fox prowling near
Emily's goslings, he tries to
warn the geese: "The fox
has big ears, bright eyes,
and sleek, shiny fur," he
says. But Emily's silly
neighbor, Lulu, thinks
George is the fox!

Related Books
Mouse Mess
by Linnea Riley
ill. by Linnea Riley
Scholastic, Inc., 1997

Frederick
(Caldecott Honor)
by Leo Lionni
ill. by Leo Lionni
Alfred A. Knopf, 1973

Imagining/Writing
There is a family of mice
living under the floor of
your room. When you're not
there, they sneak up and
carry home some of the
things you've forgotten to
put away. Which of your
forgotten things do you
think the mice like best?

13 Glue a mini pom-pom nose over the knot.

14 Trace around the eyebrow pattern twice and cut out.

15 Glue an eyebrow on the upper half of each eye.

Space Mobiles

Preparation

Cut the purple and tan sheets of foam in half. Cut the gray into twelve 6" × 12" (15cm × 31cm) pieces. Cut the black and red into twelve 1½" × 12" (4mm × 31cm) pieces. Cut ten 4-yard (1.2m) pieces of black string.

   Trace the patterns from page 118 onto cardboard and cut out three of each. Remove the outsides of the embroidery hoops and set them aside for another project.

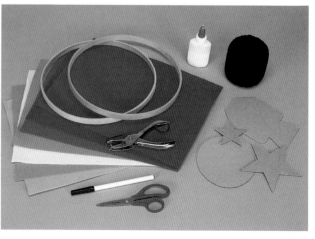

Using the Patterns

Patterns are on page 118. Use the large star pattern to cut four stars from the tan; use the small star pattern to cut eight stars from the purple. Cut just inside the pen lines. Use the circle pattern to cut one sun from the orange, one earth from the blue and one moon from the gray. Use the spaceship pattern to cut one spaceship from the gray. Cut the red into two pieces down the length, using a zigzag pattern so that each piece looks like a row of teeth. Clip between each tooth within ⅛" (3mm) of the straight edge, being careful not to cut all the way through.

1 Stars
Glue the purple stars to both sides of the tan stars.

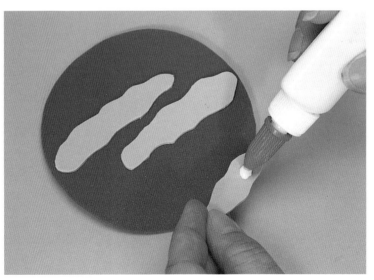

2 Sun
Bend a red strip around the edge of the front of the sun, teeth to the outside, and trim to fit. Glue in place. Glue the other strip around the edge of the back of the circle. Set aside to dry.

3 Earth and Moon
Cut gray clouds from the scraps to decorate both sides of the Earth. Use the paper punch to cut purple craters to decorate both sides of the moon.

4 Spaceship
Cut thin strips down the length of the black foam to decorate both sides of the spaceship. Cut two triangles for the windows, and cut the tips off of the tops. Glue and set aside to dry.

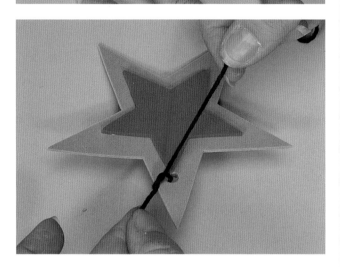

5 Punch a hole for hanging in the top of each piece. Divide the black string into twelve 12" (31cm) pieces. Tie one end of a string to each foam shape with a double overhand knot.

6 Tie the other ends of the string to the embroidery hoop, spacing the shapes evenly around the hoop with a star between every shape. Tie the remaining strings next to the star strings. Pull these four strings up, making sure the hoop hangs evenly, and tie together in a loop with an overhand knot to hang.

Featured Book
The Worst Band in the Universe
by Graeme Base
ill. by Graeme Base
Harry N. Abrams, 1999

What do you do if you're a young musician and no one on your planet appreciates your music? You take off for Sector 84 and enter the "Worst Band in the Universe Contest." First prize? Fame, fortune, and a free trip to fabulous Alpha 10.

Related Books
Alistair in Outer Space
by Marilyn Sadler
ill. by Roger Bollen
Prentice-Hall, 1984

June 29,1999
by David Wiesner
ill. by David Wiesner
Houghton Mifflin Co., 1995

Imagining/Writing
You are sitting on a park bench, sharing a bag of popcorn with the birds, when a spaceship lands on the grass in front of you. The door opens and a strange-looking being steps out. Luckily, you always carry your universal translator with you.

Flowerpot Pincushions

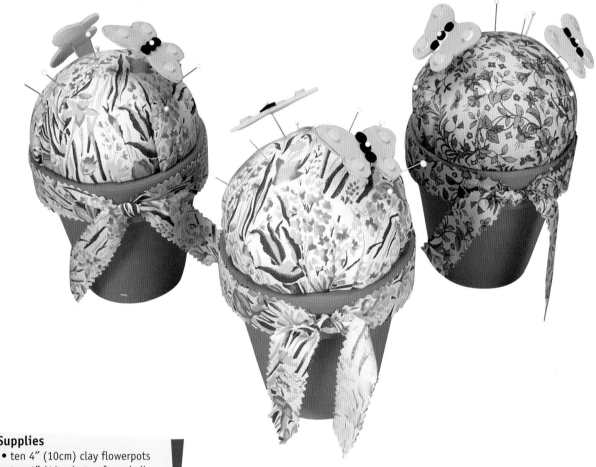

Supplies
- ten 4" (10cm) clay flowerpots
- ten 4" (10cm) styrofoam balls
- 1⅛ yards (1.1m) of 45" (1.1m) flowered cotton fabric
- ⅔ yard (61cm) of 60" (1.5m) polyester batting
- three 9" × 12" (23cm × 31cm) foam sheets: 1 black, 1 peach and 1 yellow
- 100 round-head pins
- 10 rubber bands
- 10 pairs of scissors
- 10 ballpoint pens
- 5 bottles of white glue
- 5 paper punches
- pinking shears
- cardboard

Each participant should have a flowerpot, a styrofoam ball, one 11¼" × 12" (29cm × 31cm) piece of fabric, one 11" × 12" (28cm × 31cm) batting piece, one 1" × 24½" (2.5cm × 62cm) fabric ribbon, three 3" × 4" (8cm × 10cm) pieces of sheet foam, ten pins and a rubber band.

Preparation

(1) Fold one yard (.9m) of fabric in thirds, in half and then in half again, and cut into twelve 11¼" × 12" (29cm × 31cm) pieces. Using pinking shears, cut six 1" (2.5cm) wide ribbons out of the rest of the fabric. Cut each ribbon in half. Trim the ends of the ribbons with pinking shears.

(2) Fold the batting in half, in half again, and then in thirds, and cut twelve 11" × 12" (28cm × 31cm) pieces. Trace the butterfly pattern from page 124 onto cardboard and cut out three. Cut each sheet of foam into twelve 3" × 4" (8cm × 10cm) pieces.

1 Center the fabric over the batting. Smooth both over the styrofoam ball.

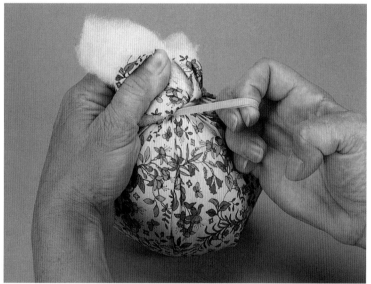

2 Tie the ends tightly with a rubberband.

3 Spread glue along the in-side of the rim of the clay pot. Press the ball firmly into the pot, rubberband end down.

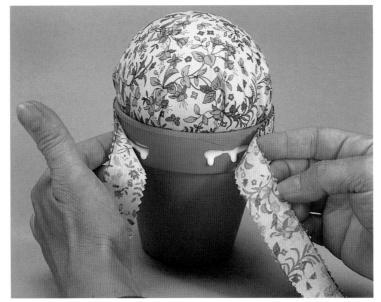

4 Spread glue along the outside of the rim of the clay pot, except for 3" (8mm) in the front. Center the middle of the ribbon opposite the front of the pot and smooth the ribbon onto the rim up to the unglued part. Leave the ends hanging in front. Let dry.

5 Trace the butterfly pattern onto the peach and yellow foam. Cut out just inside the pen lines.

6 Use the paper punch to make dots to decorate the butterflies, and then glue them in place.

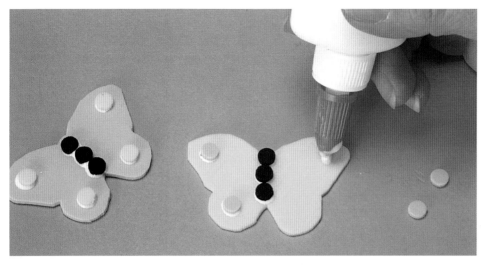

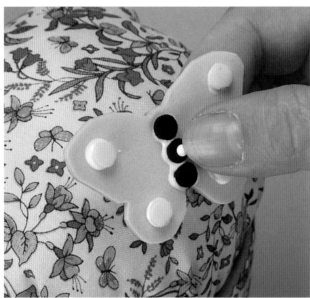

7 Stick a round-head pin through the middle of each butterfly and into the pin cushion. Stick eight more pins into the cushion. Tie the ends of the ribbon with a double overhand knot. Turn the ends so that the right side of the fabric faces the front.

Featured Book
The Gardener
by Sarah Stewart
ill. by David Small
Farrar, Straus & Giroux, 2000

Mama and Papa have to send Lydia Grace to the city to live with unsmiling Uncle Jim until there's more money coming in. But Lydia Grace has the soul of a gardener, just like her Grandma, and she's determined to make the city bloom—and maybe even make Uncle Jim smile!

Related Books
The Paradise Garden
by Colin Thompson
ill. by Colin Thompson
Alfred A. Knopf, 1998

My Day in the Garden
by Miela Ford
ill. by Anita Lobel
Greenwillow Books, 1999

Imagining/Writing
You just sat down in the garden to read when you hear someone sniffling. One of the roses on the trellis is crying. It's a good idea to be polite to roses; they have thorns. So you ask her, politely, why she is sad, and she tells you an amazing story.

No-Sew Doll Pinafores

Supplies (for 18″ dolls)
- 3 yards (2.7m) of 36″ (91cm) white felt
- eight 9″ × 12″ (23cm × 31cm) felt squares: 4 green, 2 red and 2 blue
- 5 yards (4.5m) of ⅜″ (1cm) red grosgrain ribbon
- 10 pairs of scissors
- 10 ballpoint pens
- 5 bottles of white glue
- 1 box of safety pins
- cardboard

Each participant should have two pieces of white felt: one 9″ × 24″ (23cm × 61cm) and one 9″ × 12″ (23cm × 31cm); one 4″ × 9″ (10cm × 23cm) piece of green felt, two 3″ × 6″ (8cm × 15cm) pieces of felt (one red and one blue) and one 18″ (46cm) ribbon.

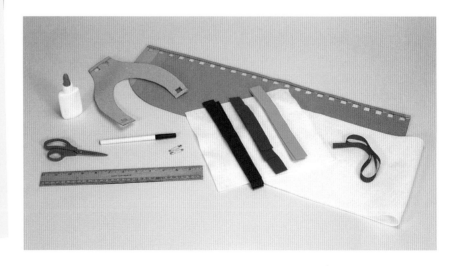

Preparation

Fold two yards of the white felt in thirds, in half and then in half again, and cut twelve 9" × 24" (23cm × 31cm) pieces. Fold the remaining yard (91cm) in thirds, in half, and then in half again, and cut twelve 9" × 12" (23cm × 31cm) pieces. Cut the green felt squares in thirds; cut the red and blue in thirds and then in half. Cut the ribbon into ten 18" (46cm) lengths.

Transfer the pattern pieces from page 119 onto cardboard. Cut out three of each pattern. Glue the long strips along the tops of the skirt patterns and the short strips along the bottoms and strap ends of the yoke patterns.

1 Trace around the skirt pattern on the 9" × 24" (23cm × 31cm) piece of white felt, being careful to mark both sides of each notch, but not the tops or bottoms of the notches.

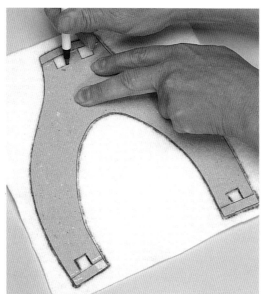

2 Trace around the yoke pattern on the 9" × 12" (23cm × 31cm) piece of white felt, also marking only the sides of each notch. Cut around the outside of each piece, just inside the pen lines.

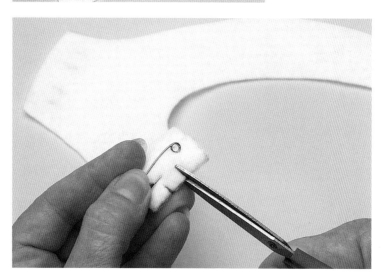

3 Fold the top edge of the skirt so that all the ½" (1.3cm) notches are folded in half. Secure with safety pins. Clip the notches open, being very careful not to cut through the edge. Fold the bottom edge and strap ends of the yoke, secure with safety pins, and clip the notches.

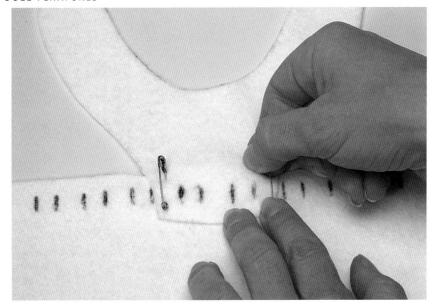

4 Remove the safety pins and unfold. Fold the skirt lengthwise to find the middle. Mark with a safety pin. Fold the yoke bottom and mark the center with a safety pin. Center the bottom of the yoke behind the center top edge of the skirt, and line up the yoke and skirt notches. Secure the yoke to the skirt with safety pins.

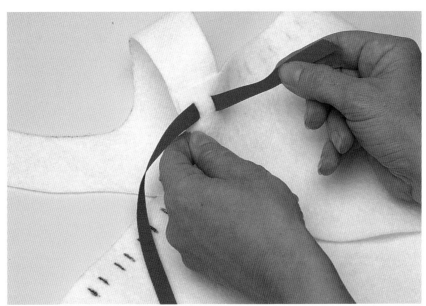

5 Bend the skirt around in a circle and place one yoke strap under each end, matching the notches with the last notches on each end of the skirt. Secure with safety pins. Thread the ribbon through the notches, securing the yoke to the skirt as you thread.

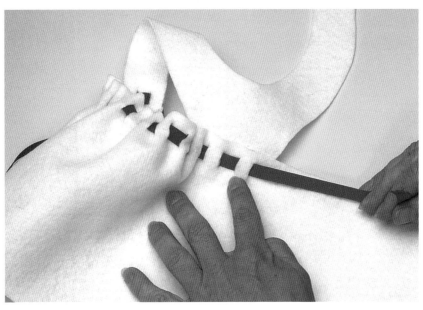

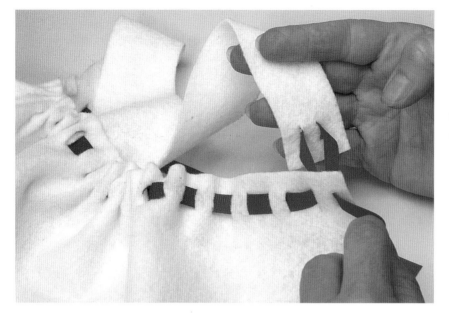

6 Pull the skirt in to gather it. Remove the safety pins. Clip the ends of the ribbon on the diagonal.

7 Decorate the skirt with flowers and leaves cut from the colored felt. For flowers, cut pieces about 1″ (2.5cm) square out of the red and blue felt, and then fold on the diagonal. Clip small triangles out of both ends of the fold. Unfold, fold on the other diagonal and clip.

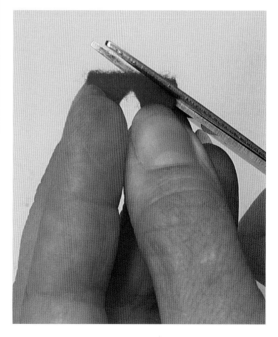

Featured Book
The Hidden House
by Martin Waddell
ill. by Angela Barrett
Candlewick Press, 1997

The three dolls, Maisie, Ralph and Winnaker, didn't say anything when the old man who carved them went away one day and never came back. Dolls don't talk, of course, but as they sat on the window ledge and watched the trees and bushes and mold and spiders change the house, they must have been sad. Then one day a man breaks through the underbrush and finds the deserted house. He brings his family, and his daughter finds the dolls.

Related Books
William's Doll
by Charlotte Zolotow
ill. by William Pene Du Bois
HarperCollins, 1985

Elisabeth
by Claire A. Nivola
ill. by Claire A. Nivola
Farrar, Straus & Giroux, 1997

Imagining/Writing
Grandmother's doll is a beautiful porcelain doll in a black lace dress. She sits on the top shelf of the tall armoire, guarding the rosebud china. You know you aren't supposed to touch her, but suddenly you find yourself perched on the top of a stool, reaching out to lift her down.

For leaves, cut pieces about 1" (2.5cm) square out of the green felt. Fold on the diagonal and cut into two triangles. Cut a curved notch in the shortest side of the triangle.

8 Glue leaves and flowers onto the pinafore in a pattern.

Under-the-Sea Mobiles

Supplies
- 10 lbs. (4.5kg) of flour (20 cups)
- 10 cups (3kg) of salt (four 26 oz. boxes)
- ten 4" (10cm) round aluminum baking pans
- 40 yards (36.6m) of white string
- aluminum foil
- cardboard
- two 4" (10cm) round styrofoam balls
- plastic knives
- soda straws
- 10 small scallop shells
- 5 rulers
- 3 star-shaped cookie cutters
- large bowl
- large mixing spoon
- one-cup measure
- 3 rolls of clear tape
- plastic wrap

Each participant should have one batch of salt dough: 2 cups (240g) of flour, 1 cup (288g) of salt and 1 scant cup (.2l) of water; one aluminum baking pan, two pieces of cardboard and shared aluminum foil.

Preparation

Mix five double batches of salt dough: 4 cups (480g) flour, 2 cups (576g) salt and 2 scant cups (.4l) water. Knead until smooth. Divide into single batches, wrap in plastic wrap and refrigerate until needed (dough should be made only a few hours ahead). Cut the string into 4-yard (3.6m) hanks.

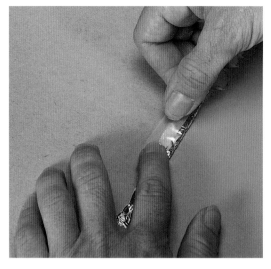

1 Crinkle two pieces of aluminum foil and then open them flat. Cover two pieces of cardboard with the crinkled aluminum foil (at least 2 square feet). Tape the edges of the foil to the back of the cardboard.

2 Using the styrofoam ball as a mold, push up the bottom of the aluminum pan until it is rounded. Pat down the edges until they are even.

3 Roll dough into a fat sausage. Divide it into thirds.

4 With the palms of your hands and your fingers, pat the first third into a 7" (18cm) circle. Pat it down on the foil to pick up the texture. Turn it over and pat gently on the other side. If the dough starts to get too smooth, crinkle an extra piece of foil and pat the top of the dough with it.

5 Invert the rounded aluminum pan on one corner of the foil-covered cardboard. Lower the circle of dough over it, centering it so the edges are even.

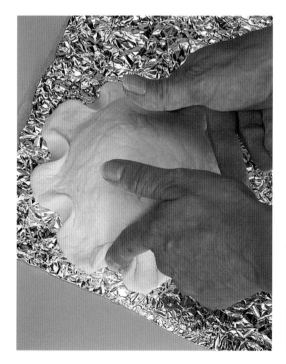

6 Push in edges with your fingertips, making a border of eight curves.

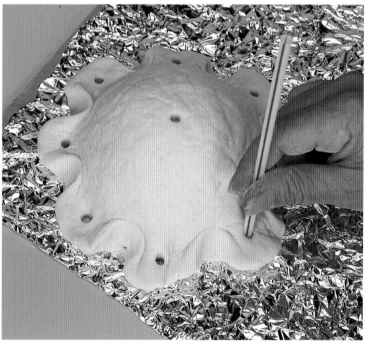

7 Lower the soda straw into the center of each curve and twist to remove a circle of dough. Blow the dough plug out of the straw after each twist and save it. Also twist a hole in the center top of the jellyfish.

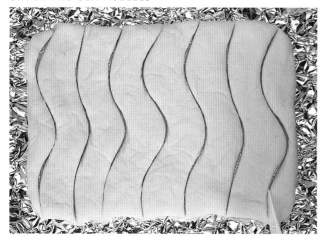

8 Pat the second third of the dough into a 5″ × 7″ (13cm × 18cm) rectangle. Pat onto the foil to pick up the texture. Turn it over and pat the other side gently. Using the plastic knife, cut wavy lines down the width of the rectangle, about ¾″ (2cm) apart, until you have six pieces of seaweed.

9 Remove the dough from each side and twist a hole in each end of each piece of seaweed. Save the scraps and plugs.

10 Pat the last third into a 5″ × 7″ (13cm × 18cm) rectangle. Pat onto the foil for texture. Cut out four starfish. Roll scraps into a ball, pat out to the same thickness, and cut out two more starfish. Twist holes in the top and bottom of each starfish. Save the plugs.

11 Roll the scraps and plugs into a ball, divide it in half and roll into two 3″ (8cm) sausages. Divide the first sausage into quarters and then in half again.

12 Roll each piece into a ball. Press each piece onto the back of a scallop shell. Turn the piece over and press lightly again to get texture on both sides. Twist a hole near the top. Save the plugs.

13 Divide the second 3" (8cm) sausage into quarters and then into quarters again. Roll each piece into a ball and flatten slightly. Twist a hole in each bead. Roll the plugs together and make as many beads out of them as you can.

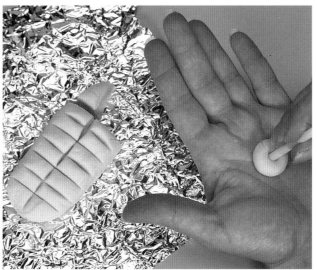

Imagining/Writing
You bring a goldfish home from the fair and make her a home in a bowl of water on your bedside table. But she tells you that you must take her back to the ocean. And if you do, she will show you a sunken ship full of treasure.

14 At home, bake on the aluminum-covered cardboard (cardboard will not burn) for 8 hours at 200°F (93°C). String a bead below and above the center hole in the jellyfish, and tie a loop to hang it. Tie the sea creatures and remaining beads from the holes in the edges of the jellyfish. The mobile can be painted or decorated with crayon designs.

Refrigerator Pigs

Supplies

- 2 or 3 pairs of pantyhose (pink, white or light tan)
- one 12 oz. (340g) bag of polyester stuffing
- 100 small rubber bands
- one 9" × 12" (23cm × 31cm) felt square in pink, white or tan (to match pantyhose)
- four 9" × 12" (23cm × 31cm) felt squares in at least two bright colors (or scraps)
- twenty ⅛" (3mm) glue-on googly eyes
- 10 square inches (25 square cm) of magnet sheet or 10 dot magnets
- 10 pairs of scissors
- 10 ballpoint pens
- 5 bottles of white glue
- cardboard

Each participant should have a 6" (15cm) piece of pantyhose, ten rubber bands, one 3" × 4" (8cm × 10cm) piece of pink, tan or white felt, two 3" × 4" (8cm × 10cm) pieces of bright-colored felt (or scraps), two googly eyes, one magnet square and shared stuffing.

Preparation

Cut stocking legs into ten 6" (15cm) pieces, avoiding runs and holes. Fold and cut the felt in half, in half again and then in thirds to make 3" × 4" (8cm × 10cm) pieces. Trace patterns from page 123 for the collar, hat and flower onto cardboard and cut out three of each. If using a magnet sheet, cut into 1" (2.5cm) squares.

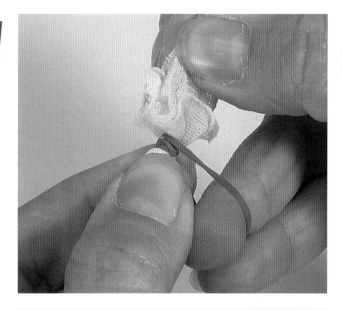

1 Gather bottom edge of stocking piece together and tie tightly with a rubber band.

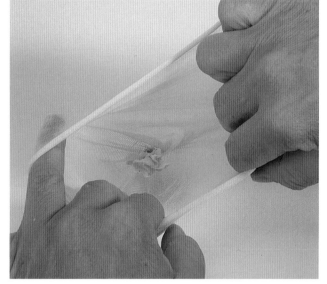

2 Turn inside out.

3 Pack with a ball of stuffing about the size of a base-ball.

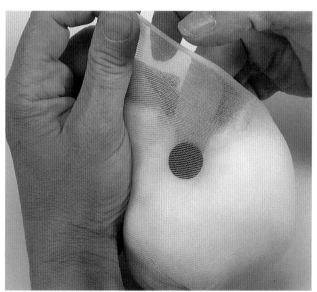

4 Slip magnet down the back side of the ball.

5 Tie off the top edge with a rubber band. Trim the edges close to the rubber band.

6 Pinch off about one-fourth at the top of the ball for the head. Tie off loosely with a rubber band.

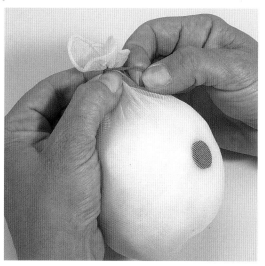

7 Pinch off a piece the size of a marble at the front of the head for the snout. Tie off loosely with a rubber band.

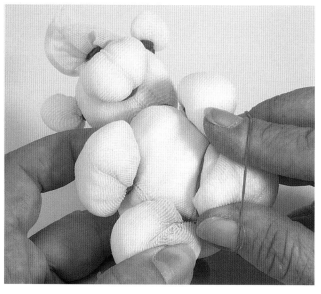

8 Pinch off a piece the size of a navy bean on each side of the top of the head for the ears. Tie off tightly with rubber bands.

9 Pinch off four pieces about the size of marbles at the four corners of the front of the body for feet. Tie off loosely with rubber bands.

10 Draw around the patterns for the collar and flower on the first color of felt and cut out, being careful to cut just inside the pen lines. Trace and cut the hat from the second color of felt.

11 Cut thirteen small dots to decorate the flower and collar and glue them in place. Slip the collar over the pig's head, glue the hat on between the ears and glue the flower on the hat.

12 Cut out two tiny circles from red or pink felt and glue on the pig's nose. Glue on two googly eyes.

13 Cut a small spiral tail of pink, white or tan felt. Glue over the rubber band on the pig's bottom.

Candy Corn Bracelets

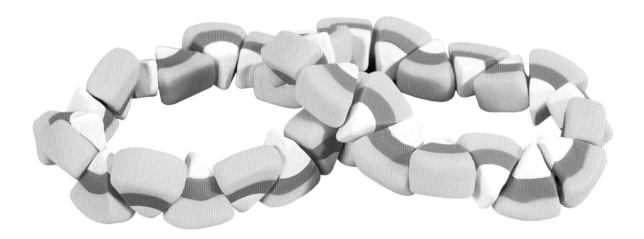

Supplies

- twelve 2-oz. (56g) slabs of polymer clay: 5 yellow, 4 orange and 3 white
- 7 yards (6.4m) of black elastic cord
- 30 wooden skewers
- cardboard
- clay rollers
- clay blades
- 5 rulers

To make two bracelets, each participant should have 2 quarters of yellow clay, 1½ quarters of orange clay, one quarter of white clay, two 12" (31cm) lengths of black elastic cord, three skewers and one piece of cardboard.

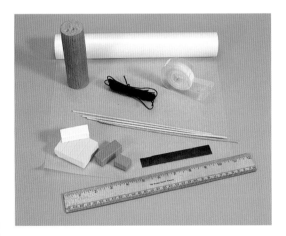

Preparation

Cut the clay into quarters. Cut five of the orange quarters in half. Cut the elastic cord into 12" (31cm) lengths.

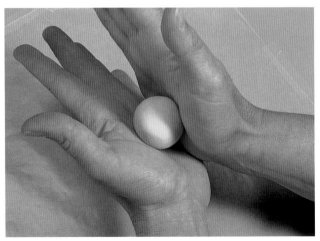

1 Knead the white clay in your hands until it is warm and pliable.

2 Roll into a 2″ (5cm) sausage, making sure the thickness is even. Set aside.

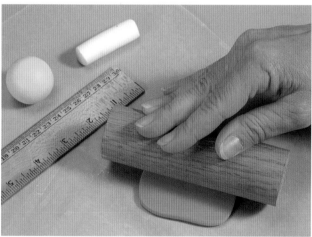

3 Knead the orange clay. Roll into a 2″ (5cm) sausage. Use the roller and your fingertips to flatten the sausage into a sheet 2″ (5cm) wide and long enough to wrap around the white sausage.

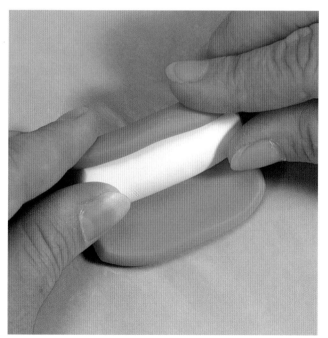

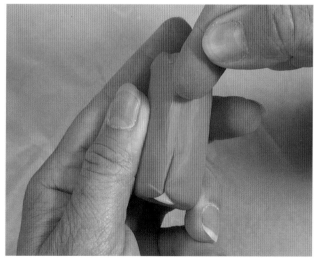

4 Wrap the white sausage with the orange and roll it a few times to make sure the orange adheres to the white. If the sausage starts to get longer than 2″ (5cm), pat it back to the correct length.

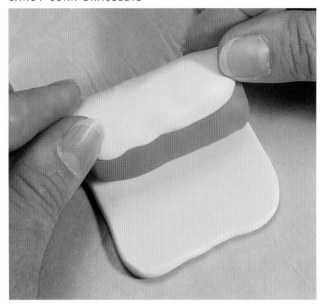

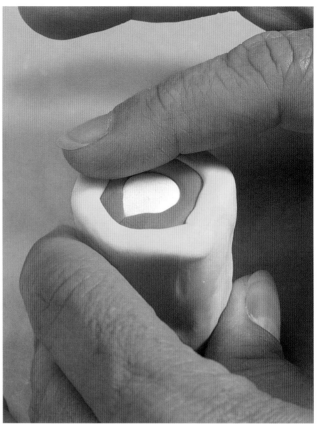

5 Knead the yellow clay and roll into a 2″ (5cm) sausage. Use the roller and your fingertips to flatten the sausage into a sheet 2″ (5cm) wide and long enough to wrap around the white and orange sausage. Wrap the white and orange sausage with the yellow and roll it a few times to make sure the yellow adheres to the white and orange. If the sausage starts to get longer than 2″ (5cm), pat it back to the correct length.

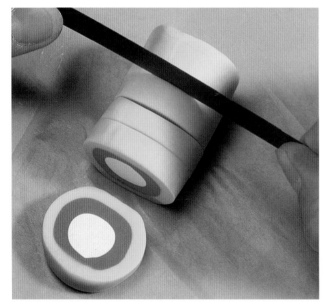

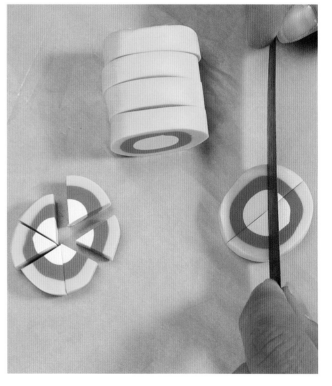

6 Using the clay blade, slice the sausage in half and then in thirds, making six wheels. Then slice each wheel like a pie into six equal wedges. Be careful to hold the blade only by the dull edge and slice straight down.

7 Using the sharp end of the skewer, bore a hole through the side of each piece of candy corn. Twist the skewer as it goes in so that you don't mash your shape.

8 Thread twelve pieces of candy corn on each skewer.

At Home
Carry your skewered candy corn home on a piece of cardboard and bake in the oven for 20 minutes at 265°F (129°C) (the cardboard will not burn). When cool, remove the skewers and thread half the candy corn on each elastic cord. Tie the ends together with an overhand knot. Give one bracelet to a friend.

Moon and Stars Lanterns

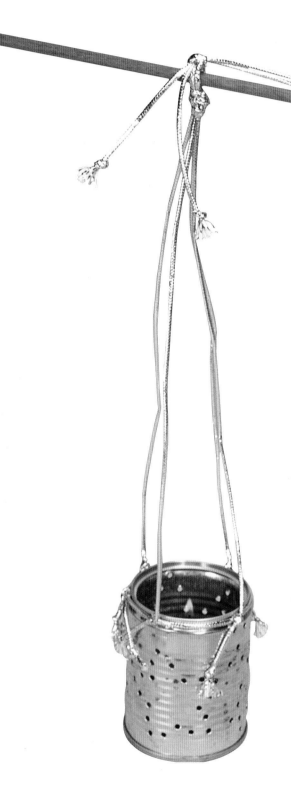

Supplies
- ten 6-oz. (170g) pop-top fruit cans
- ten 3' (91cm) long, ¼" (6mm) wooden dowels
- 10 red votive candles
- 25 yards (23m) of silver cord
- 10 sheets of copy paper
- 10 small terrycloth towels
- 10 pairs of scissors
- 10 permanent red markers
- 3 rolls of clear tape
- 10 hammers
- 10 large nails
- hot water

Each participant should have one pop-top can, one wooden dowel, one red candle, one 2-yard (1.8m) piece of silver cord, one 18" (46cm) piece of silver cord and one paper pattern.

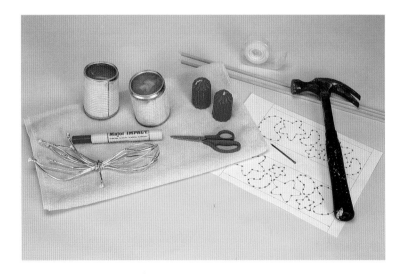

Preparation

Remove labels from cans, fill with water and freeze. Cut ten 2-yard (1.8m) pieces of cord and ten 18" (46cm) pieces. Make ten copies of the moon-and-stars pattern from page 120.

1 Cut out a moon-and-stars pattern and tape it around the can. Fold the towel in quarters and position the can firmly in the center.

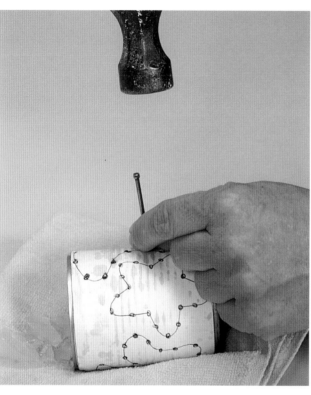

2 Use the hammer and nail to make holes through the dots on the pattern and through the can. Turn the can as you work, so that you are always hammering straight down from the top. When you are finished, remove the pattern and discard. Run hot water in the can to remove the remaining ice. Dry the can with the towel.

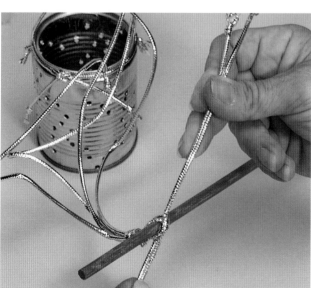

3 Cut the 2-yard (1.8m) piece of cord into quarters. Tape the pieces of cord to the outside of the can, dividing it into quarters. One end of each cord should reach down to the middle of the outside of the can. Tie the 18" (46cm) cord tightly around the top of the can, just under the lip, with a double overhand knot. Remove the tape, bring each cord up, and tie around the top cord with a double overhand knot. Trim the ends of the cords. Tie the ends with overhand knots if they unravel easily. Color the dowel red with the marker. Bring the cords up, and tie all of them together with one overhand knot about 3" (8cm) from the ends. Divide the cords into two groups and tie them around one end of the dowel with a double overhand knot. Trim the ends. Insert the red candle in the lantern.

Featured Book

Moon Festival
by Ching Yeung Russell
ill. by C. Zhong-Yuan Zhang
Boyds Mill Press, 1997

On the day of the Moon Festival, Chinese children walk back and forth in front of the bakery to catch the fragrance of baking moon cakes, filled with bean paste and salty duck-egg yolks. Then they admire the painting of Chang O, rising toward the moon with her white rabbit in her arms. Later they will light their lanterns and dance in the silver moonlight.

Related Books

Rabbit Mooncakes
by Hoong Yee Lee Krakauer
ill. by Hoong Yee Lee Karkauer
Little, Brown & Co., 1994

Moon Lady
by Amy Tan
ill. by Gretchen Schields
Simon & Schuster, 1995

Imagining/Writing

Make up a moon festival of your own. What special foods will you eat? When will you light your lantern? Will you dance or sing, or tell stories about the moon?

Folded Paper Birds

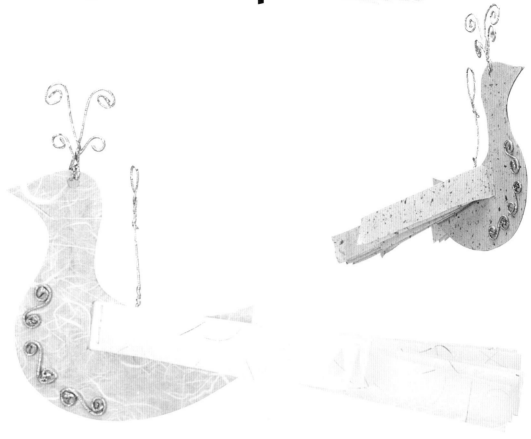

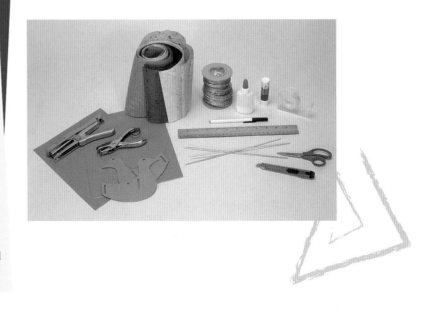

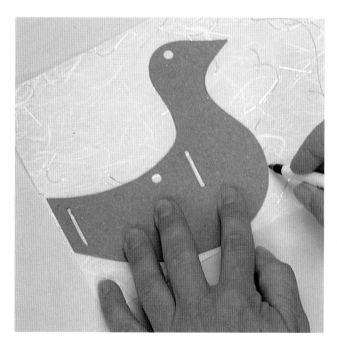

1 First, trace the bird pattern onto cardboard and cut it out. An adult should use the mat knife to cut the slits. Punch holes with the paper punch. Then trace the cardboard pattern onto a 6" × 12" (15cm × 31cm) piece of handmade paper twice, facing opposite directions. Cut out, slightly outside the pen lines. Cut out slits slightly inside the pen lines.

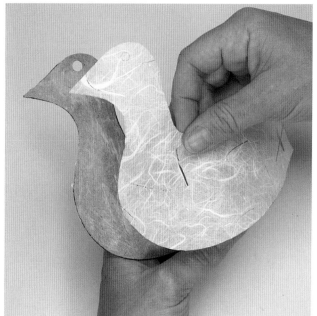

2 Paint one side of the cardboard with the gluestick. Smooth one paper bird over the cardboard with the side with the pen lines facing down. Trim the edges as necessary. Turn the cardboard over and paint the other side with the gluestick. Smooth the second paper bird over it with the pen lines facing down. Trim as needed.

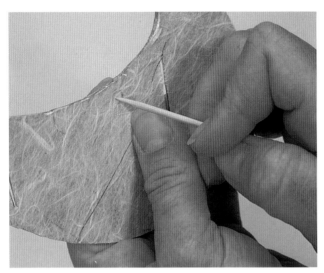

3 Find the punch holes with a toothpick and repunch them.

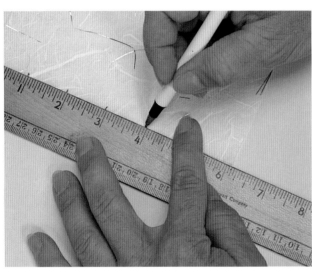

4 Mark the short edges of two 6" × 12" (15cm × 31cm) pieces of paper with small dots at every inch (2.5cm).

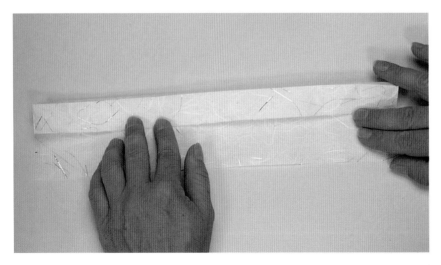

5 Fold papers, accordion style, into 1" (2.5cm) folds, using marks as guides.

6 Fold each stack in half length-wise. Hold one folded stack with side edges down and insert it into tail slit. Fasten with two staples about ⅛″ (3mm) from slit.

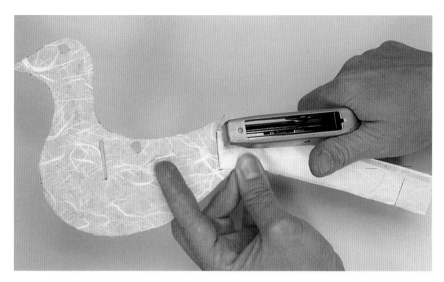

7 Holding the second stack with side edges down, insert it into wing slit, facing the tail.

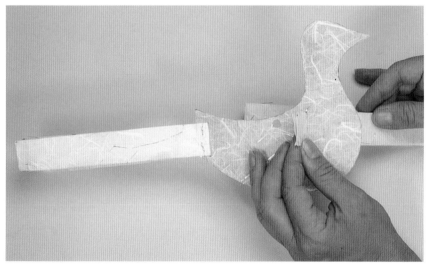

8 Fasten with two staples about ⅛″ (3mm) from slit. Bend slightly open on each side.

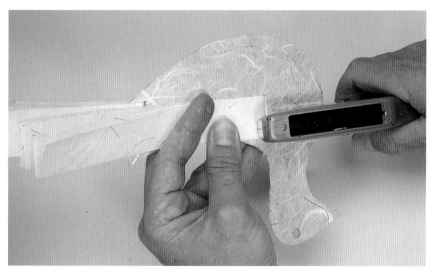

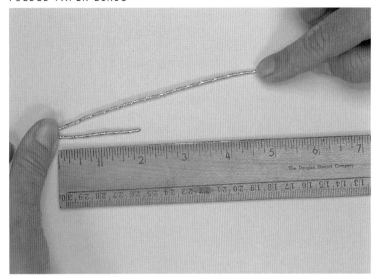

9 Cut wired cord into two 7" (18cm) pieces, one 6" (15cm) piece, and six 3" (8cm) pieces.

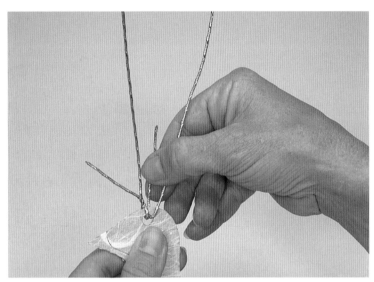

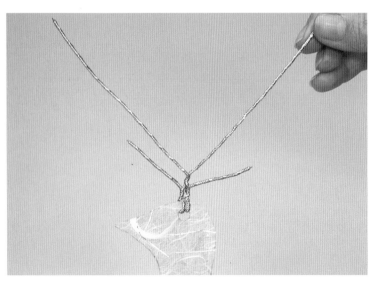

10 Bend up 2″ (5cm) on one end of each 7" (18cm) piece. Thread through head hole, with the 2″ (5cm) ends facing front and back.

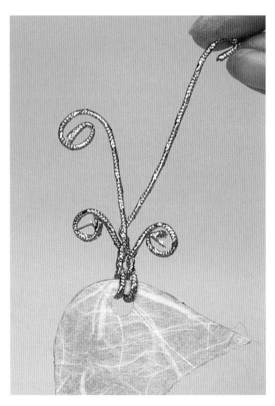

11 Twist each piece once, returning the shorter pieces to the front and back. Twist the middle pieces together once.

12 Bend the end of each into a spiral facing front or back. Bend the wired cord around a toothpick to start the center of each spiral.

13 Bend ½" (13mm) up on one end of the 6" (15cm) piece, and bend 2" (5cm) up on the other end. Thread the ½" (13mm) end through the body hole and twist. Twist the other end, leaving a ¾" (2cm) loop.

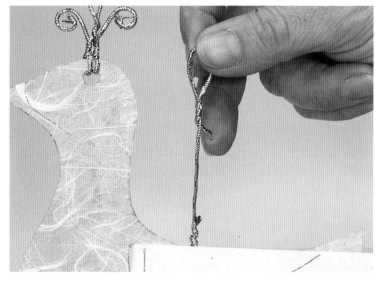

14 Make six double spirals out of the 3" (8cm) pieces. Spread white glue on one side of them and glue them to the edge of the chest and neck of both sides of the bird. Adjust the tightness of the hanging wire, or add more double spirals if necessary, until the bird's wings and tail hang fairly level.

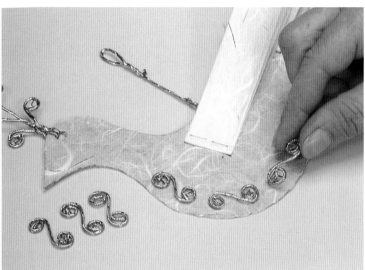

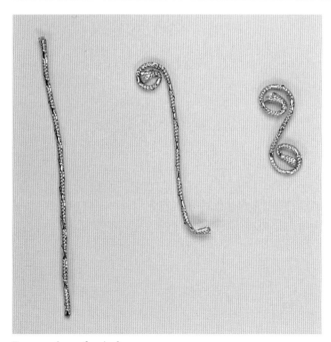

Progression of spirals.

Featured Book
The Paper Crane
(Reading Rainbow)
by Molly Bang
ill. by Molly Bang
Morrow, William & Co.,
1987

One evening an old, tattered man comes into a restaurant. And though he has no money for food, the owner serves him a magnificent meal. To reward his host, the old man makes him a crane out of folded white paper. When the restaurant owner claps his hands, the crane springs to life and dances around the dining room.

Related Books
Tree of Cranes
by Allen Say
ill. by Allen Say
Houghton Mifflin Co., 1991

Sadako
by Eleanor Coerr
ill. by Ed Young
Putnam Publishing, 1997

Imagining/Writing
The evil Lord of Rockcliff Tower says he will never let you go, since your father cannot come up with the ransom. But you have begged the servant who brings your meager dinner for a piece of white paper, which you have folded into a tiny paper bird. Now if only you can remember the spell that will bring the bird to life!

Lizard Mola Book Covers

Supplies

- 3 yards (2.75m) of red felt
- five 9″ × 12″ (23cm × 31cm) squares of black felt
- five 9″ × 12″ (23cm × 31cm) squares of yellow felt
- three 3½–4 oz. (100g) skeins of black acrylic yarn
- 10 pairs of scissors
- 10 ballpoint pens
- 5 bottles of white glue
- 5 staplers
- mat knife
- cardboard

Each participant should have one 12″ × 18″ (31cm × 46cm) piece of red felt, one 9″ × 12″ (23cm × 31cm) piece of red felt, one 6″ × 9″ (15cm × 23cm) piece of red felt, one 6″ × 9″ piece of black felt, one 6″ × 9″ piece of yellow felt and one 1-yard (91cm) piece and one 11-yard (10.1m) piece of black yarn.

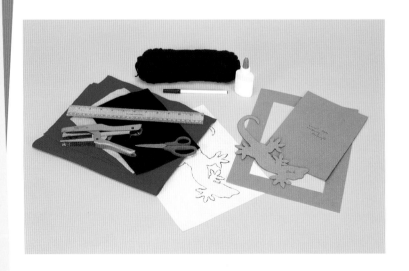

Preparation

Cut a 9″ × 12″ (23cm × 31cm) rectangle of cardboard. Cut a 6″ × 9″ (15cm × 23cm) rectangle out of the middle. Transfer the lizard pattern from page 122 onto cardboard, and cut three. Use the mat knife to cut between the toes. Cut ten 12″ × 18″ (31cm × 46cm) rectangles from the red felt. Next, cut ten 9″ × 12″ (23cm × 31cm) rectangles. Cut the remaining red felt into twelve 6″ × 9″ (15cm × 23cm) rectangles. Cut the black and yellow felt squares in half to make ten 6″ × 9″ (15cm × 23cm) pieces of each. Cut ten 1-yard (91cm) pieces of yarn and ten 11-yard (10.1m) pieces of yarn.

1 On the 12″ × 18″ (31cm × 46cm) piece of red felt, trace around the 6″ × 9″ (15cm × 23cm) centering rectangle on the back side of the cover's front.

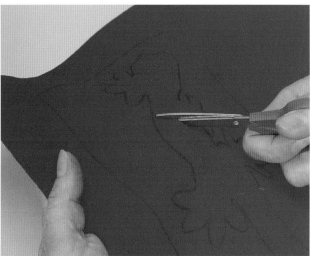

2 Center the lizard pattern in the centering rectangle, nose facing to the right. Trace around the lizard and cut it out, being careful to cut just inside the pen lines.

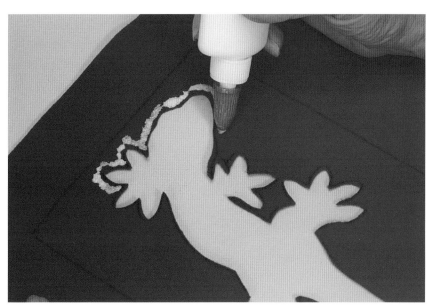

3 Spread glue along the edges of the lizard outline and along the inside edges of the centering rectangle.

4 Center a 6″ × 9″ (15cm × 23cm) piece of black felt over the centering rectangle and press down firmly along the glue lines.

5 Turn the cover to the right side and cut a slit in the middle of the lizard's belly through the black felt. Cut around the lizard outline, about ¼″ (6mm) from the red felt.

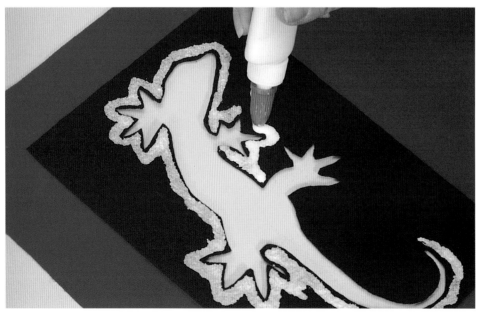

6 Turn the cover to the back side. Spread glue along the edges of the black lizard outline and along the outside edges of the black felt rectangle.

7 Center the yellow 6″ × 9″ (15cm × 23cm) rectangle over the black, and press down firmly along the glue lines. Turn the cover to the right side and cut a slit in the middle of the lizard's belly through the yellow felt. Cut around the lizard outline, about ¼″ (6mm) from the black felt.

8 Turn the cover to the back side. Spread glue along the edges of the yellow lizard outline and along the outside edges of the yellow felt rectangle. Center the red 6″ × 9″ (15cm × 23cm) rectangle over the yellow and press down firmly along the glue lines.

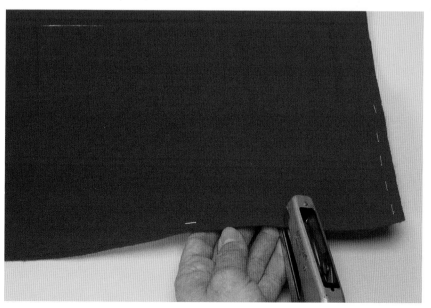

9 Cut the red 9″ × 12″ (23cm × 31cm) felt rectangle in half, widthwise. Lay the 4½″ × 12″ (11cm × 31cm) rectangles on either end of the back of the cover. Staple to the cover front around the outside edges, about ¼″ (6mm) from the edge.

Featured Book
The Iguana Brothers: A Tale of Two Lizards
by Tony Johnston
ill. by Mark Teague
Scholastic, Inc., 1995

Dom and Tom are the iguana brothers and, like many brothers, they argue endlessly about what iguanas can and cannot do. Can iguanas eat something other than disgusting bugs? Can iguanas really be dinosaurs? And can brother iguanas be friends, even though they are also brothers?

Related Books
The Salamander Room
by Anne Mazer
ill. by Steve Johnson
Alfred A. Knopf, 1994

A Color of His Own
by Leo Lionni
ill. by Leo Lionni
Alfred A. Knopf, 1997

Imagining/Writing
You have a salamander who changes color with everything he touches, which makes him a very good spy. This is a very good thing, because you're convinced that your babysitter, Ms. Axeheart, is a dangerous criminal!

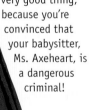

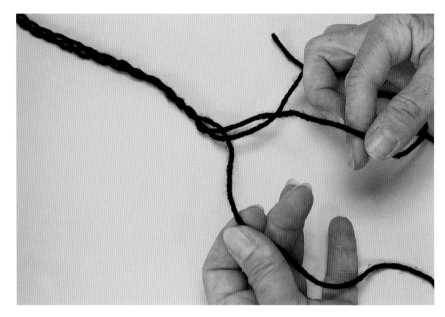

10 Using the 1-yard (91cm) piece of yarn, cut eleven more 1-yard lengths. Braid four lengths (using three pieces for each), ending with an overhand knot about 1" (2.5cm) from the end.

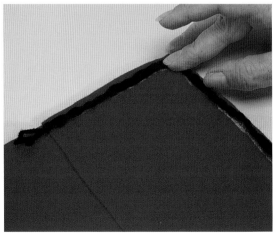

11 Draw a line of glue around the front edges of the cover, about ¼" (6mm) from the edge. Press one braid into the glue, starting at the upper left-hand corner, going across the top and ending at the lower right-hand corner. Press a second braid from the lower right-hand corner, going across the bottom and ending at the upper left-hand corner. Retie the ends and trim if necessary. Open the cover and use the remaining braids to trim the edges of the end flaps. Retie and trim the ends if necessary.

Fabric Maché Bowls

Supplies
- ten 12" (31cm) balloons
- twelve ⅓-yard (31cm) pieces of 45" (1.1m) wide flowered or patterned cotton fabric
- ⅔-yard (61cm) of 45" wide black cotton fabric
- 20 sheets of copy paper
- 10 pieces of cardboard
- 5-lb. (2.3kg) bag of flour
- 200 safety pins
- 10 pairs of scissors
- 3 rolls of clear tape
- several large bowls
- wire whisk
- 1 set of measuring cups
- yardstick (1m measure)
- water

Each participant should have one 12" (31cm) balloon, twelve 6" × 6" (15cm × 15cm) pieces of colored fabric, one 6" × 12" (15cm × 31cm) piece of black fabric, two paper patterns, one piece of cardboard and shared flour paste.

Preparation

Cut fabric widths to 36" (91cm). Cut each piece of the colored fabric in half, in half again and then in thirds, making twelve 6" × 6" (15cm × 15cm) squares. Cut the black fabric in half, in half again and then in thirds to make twelve 6" × 12" (15cm × 31cm) pieces. Make 20 copies of the two dragonfly patterns on page 123. Measure 2½ cups (300g) flour and 3¾ cups (.9l) water into each bowl. Whisk into a smooth paste.

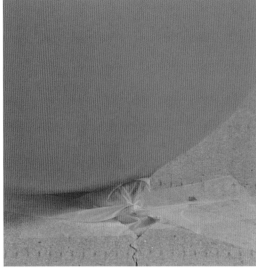

1 Blow up a balloon and tie the end. Cut a slit in a piece of cardboard and make a small square hole in the center. Slide the tied end of the balloon down the slit to the center. Tape the edges of the cardboard to the table to hold the balloon steady.

2 Cut apart the four dragonfly patterns and pin them to the black fabric with safety pins. Cut out the patterns and fabric together. Remove the patterns and discard them.

3 Cut the 6" (15cm) fabric squares in thirds and then in thirds again, making nine 2" (5cm) squares of each color.

4 Dip squares into paste, and squeeze out extra between two fingers.

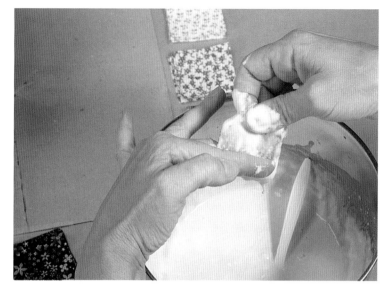

5 Paste a row of pieces around the middle of the balloon, points down, with the right side of the fabric facing the balloon. Cover the top half of the balloon with overlapping pieces, all with the right side facing the balloon.

6 Paste a row of pieces around the center of the balloon over the top of the first row with the right side of the fabric facing out. Cover the top half of the balloon with overlapping pieces, all with the right side facing out. Dip the black dragonflies in glue and paste them evenly around the bowl, heads facing down.

Featured Book
The Rag Coat
by Lauren Mills
ill. by Lauren Mills
Little, Brown & Co., 1991

Minna's papa died of the coal dust, and there's no money for a coat for Minna. Without a coat, Minna can't go to school—there's no sense in starting if she would have to stop when the weather turns cold. But the Quilting Mothers insist on donating enough of their carefully saved scraps to make Minna a rag coat. Minna picks the most worn scraps because they have the best stories about what they were and who they belonged to.

Related Books
Sweet Clara and the Freedom Quilt
(Reading Rainbow)
by Deborah Hopkinson
ill. by James Ransome
Alfred A. Knopf, 1995

Sewing Quilts
by Ann Warren Turner
ill. by Thomas B. Allen
Simon & Schuster, 1994

Imagining/Writing
Your grandmother is going to make you a quilt from scraps of some of the clothes you've worn out and outgrown. You get to help her choose the fabrics and cut the squares. Which pieces have the best memories?

At Home
Take the balloon home on the piece of cardboard and tape it to a flat surface until thoroughly dry. Break the balloon and remove it. To achieve a flat bowl bottom, set a bowl nearly as large inside and fill it with something heavy. Leave overnight.

Bubble Wands

Supplies
- 20 yards (18.3m) of aluminum clothesline wire
- four 6′ (1.8m) lengths of ¾″ (2cm) acrylic tubing (inside width)
- ten ¾″ (2cm) white plastic tube caps
- 2 boxes of colored plastic wrap: 1 green and 1 lilac
- two 12″ × 18″ (31cm × 46cm) sheets of foam: 1 green and 1 lilac
- 2 skeins of 3½–4 oz. (100g) acrylic yarn: 1 green and 1 lilac
- 1 cup (.25l) of liquid dish soap
- water
- 10 pairs of scissors
- 10 paper punches
- small handsaw
- 3 rolls of masking tape
- large, wide bowl
- large spoon
- cardboard

Each participant should have two yards of clothesline wire, one 2′ (61cm) length of acrylic tubing, two 3″ × 6″ (8cm × 15cm) pieces of sheet foam, one tube cap, eight 4′ (1.2m) pieces of yarn and shared plastic wrap.

Preparation

Saw the acrylic tubing into 2' (61cm) lengths (wrap with masking tape to mark and avoid scratches). Cut the wire into 2-yard (1.8m) lengths. Cut each sheet of foam in thirds, in half and in half again to make twelve 3" × 6" (8cm × 15cm) pieces. Trace the heart pattern from page 125 onto cardboard and cut out five.

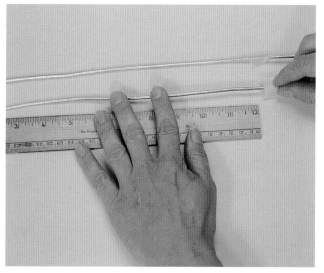

1 Bend the wire in half. Mark off 12" (31cm) from the middle with masking tape.

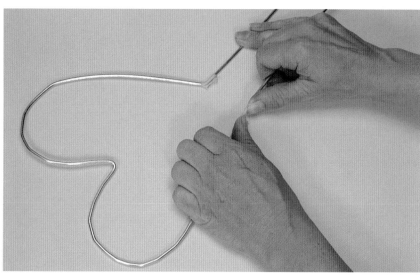

2 About 4" (10cm) from the middle, start bending the wire back, shaping it into a half-circle. Straighten out as you get to the 12" (31cm) mark, making half a heart. Bend the other side in the opposite direction, making the other half of the heart.

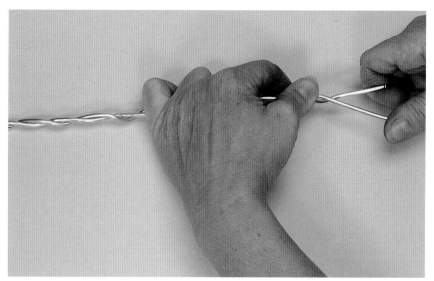

3 At the 12" (31cm) mark, twist the wires together loosely all the way to the ends.

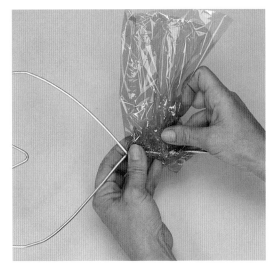

Tear off several sheets of colored plastic wrap. Wrap the twisted wire, alternating colors.

5 Stuff the wrapped wire into the acrylic tube. Add extra plastic wrap at the end if the wires don't reach all the way. Cap the bottom.

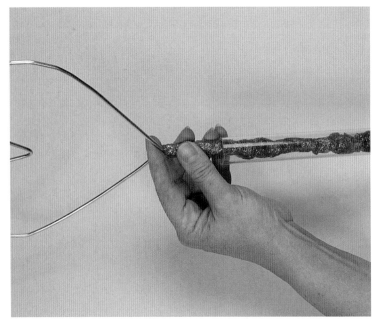

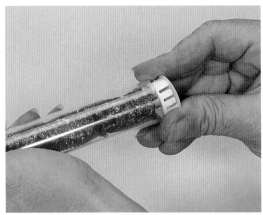

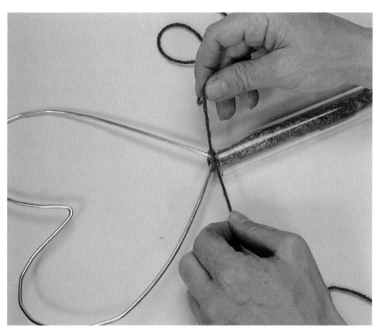

6 Trace the heart design onto the foam pieces. Cut eight of each color. Cut eight pieces of each color of yarn, making each twice the length of the tube. Fold each yarn string in half and knot it around the wire at the tip of the wire heart, alternating colors.

7 Tie four rows of square knots (see diagram on page 126) to make a cap for the top of the tube. Trim the strings to different lengths and tie a heart to the end of each with a double overhand knot.

Featured Book
King Bidgood's in the Bathtub
(Caldecott Honor)
by Audrey Wood
ill. by Don Wood
Harcourt Brace & Co., 1993

King Bidgood is in his bathtub full of bubbles, and he won't come out. He won't come out for the Knight, he won't come out for the Queen, he won't come out for the Duke, and he won't come out for the Court. Will he ever come out?

Related Books
The Bubble Factory
by Tomie De Paola
ill. by Tomie De Paola
Putnam Publishing, 1996

Casey in the Bath
by Cynthia DeFelice
ill. by Chris Demarest
Farrar, Straus & Giroux, 1998

Imagining/Writing
Just as you are about to shoot a basket out on the playground, you notice dozens of bubbles coming from behind the school building. Soon the sky is filled with bubbles. Everyone races around to the other side of the building to see what's causing them.

Making Bubbles

Fill the bowl with 2 gallons (7.5l) of water and add 1 (.25l) cup of liquid dish soap. Stir gently (avoid making bubbles). Dip the wands in the bowl and wave them gently to make giant bubbles.

Elves and Fairies

Supplies

- sixteen 2-oz. (56g) slabs of polymer clay: 5 blue, 5 purple, 3 white, 1 black, 1 brown, 1 beige
- 20 pin backs (¾" or 2cm)
- 10 pieces of cardboard
- 10 pairs of scissors
- clay blades
- 5 rulers
- clay rollers
- garlic presses
- box of toothpicks

Each participant should have a ½ slab of purple clay, ½ slab of blue clay, ¼ slab of white clay, ¹⁄₁₆ slab of black, brown and beige clay, two pin backs, black and white pressed clay strands and one piece of cardboard.

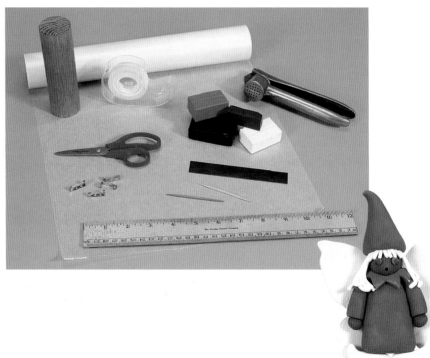

Preparation

Cut the purple and blue slabs of polymer clay in half. Cut the black, beige and brown slabs into quarters and then into quarters again. Cut ten white quarters and then cut the extra white into eighths and squeeze them through a garlic press. Squeeze black through the press the same way. Trace the butterfly wing pattern from page 125 onto cardboard and cut three.

1 **Elves:** Cut the purple clay into two pieces. Knead the first piece and roll it into a 3″ (8cm) sausage.
Fairies: Cut the blue clay into two pieces. Knead the first piece and roll it into a 1½″ (4cm) sausage.

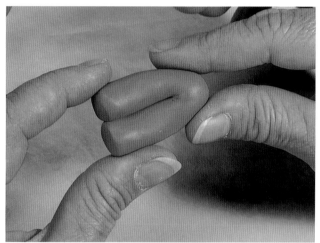

2 **Elves:** Bend the clay in half and taper the folded top. Flatten the leg bottoms slightly to widen them.
Fairies: Taper one end and flatten the other end slightly.

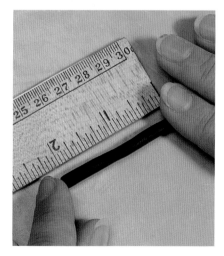 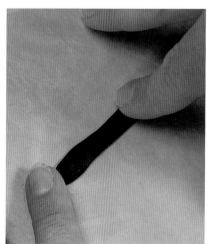

3 **Elves:** For the belt, cut a ⅛″ (3mm) slice from the end of the black piece, roll it into a 2″ (5cm) sausage and flatten it.

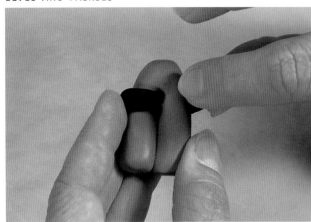

4 **Elves:** Press the belt around the middle of the folded body.

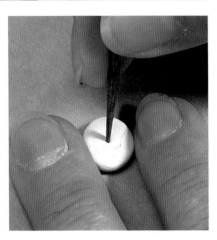

5 **Elves:** Cut a ¼" (6mm) piece from the white garlic-pressed strands, make it into an oval and flatten it. Make a hole in the middle with a toothpick.

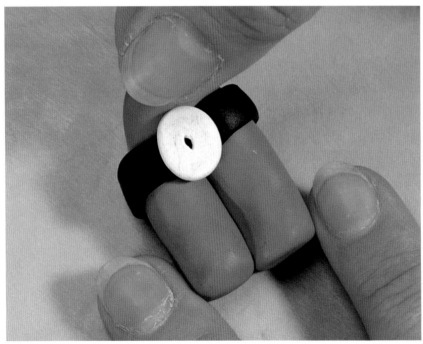

6 **Elves:** Center the piece on the front of the belt for a buckle.

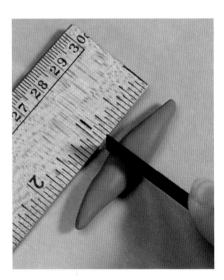

7 **Elves:** Cut the second purple piece in half and then cut one of the pieces in half again. Knead one quarter and roll it into a 2" (5cm) sausage, tapering both ends. Cut in half with a clay blade for the sleeves.
Fairies: Cut the second blue piece in half and then cut one of the halves in half again. Make the same kind of sleeves from one quarter of blue clay.

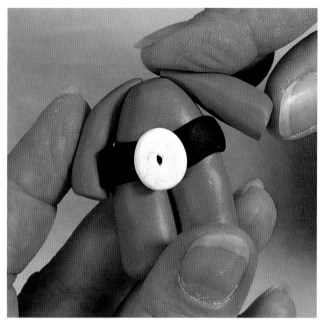

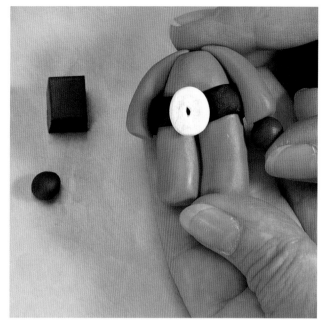

8 **Elves:** Press the tapered ends onto either side of the top of the body. Flatten the sleeve bottoms slightly to widen them.
Fairies: Follow the same process.

9 **Elves:** Choose a beige or brown piece for the heads and hands. Cut a bean-size piece and divide it into two balls. Press one onto the end of each sleeve.
Fairies: Using the beige or brown piece you have left, make the same kinds of hands and head.

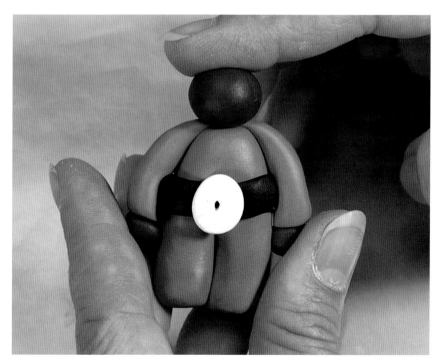

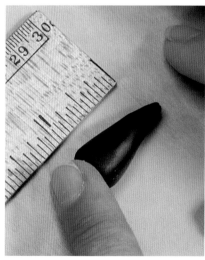

11 **Elves:** Divide the remainder of black clay in half and roll each half into a 1" (2.5 cm) sausage, tapered at one end for the shoes.

10 **Elves:** Roll the rest of the brown clay into a ball for the head and press it onto the top of the body.
Fairies: Follow the same process.

12 **Elves:** Press the fat ends to the leg bottoms with the tapers out to the sides. Curve the tapered ends up for pointed-toe shoes.

Fairies: Cut out the wings before you make the shoes. Roll the white quarter into a 3″ × 3″ (8cm × 8cm) square. Trace around the butterfly wing pattern with a toothpick and cut out with scissors. Press the wings to the center back of the dress. To make the shoes, roll the scraps into a 1″ (2.5cm) sausage and divide in half. Divide one of the pieces in half again and roll them into two 1″ (2.5cm) sausage, tapered at one end. Press the fat ends to the dress bottom with the tapers facing out at the sides. Curve the tapered ends up.

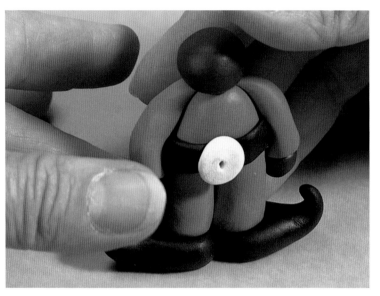

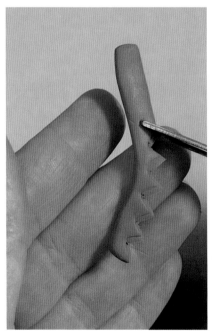

13 **Elves:** To make a collar, cut a ¼″ (6mm) slice from the remaining purple piece and roll it into a 2″ (5cm) sausage.
Fairies: Follow the same procedure using the remaining blue piece.

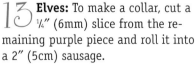

14 **Elves:** Flatten and cut tiny points with scissors along one edge.
Fairies: Follow the same process.

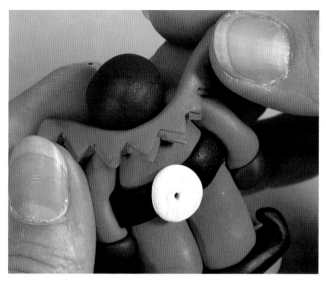

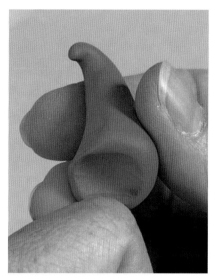

16 **Elves:** To make a hat, roll the purple half-quarter into a 1½" (4cm) sausage, tapering one end. Use your knuckle to make a bowl-shaped hollow inside the large end. Set the hat aside.

Fairies: Follow the same proce-dure using the blue clay.

15 **Elves and Fairies:** Curve the collar around the neck and press in place.

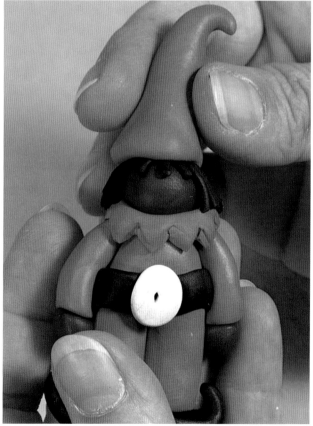

17 **Elves:** Cut small pieces from the garlic-pressed strands of black for hair. Press onto head.
Fairies: Cut pieces from the garlic-pressed strands of white for hair, short for bangs and long for the sides and back. Press onto head. Curve ends.

18 **Elves and Fairies:** Press the hat on over the hair and curve the tapered end.

Featured Book

A Fairy Went A-Marketing
by Rose Fyleman
ill. by Jamichael Henterly
Penguin USA, 1991

When fairy goes a-market-ing, she always comes home with something wonderful, but she never keeps it long. She lets her silver fish, her colored bird and her gentle mouse all go free, and she gives her winter gown to a frog to keep him warm at night.

Child of Faerie, Child of Earth
by Jane Yolen
ill. by Jane Dyer
Little, Brown & Co., 1997

Fairy Wings
by Lauren Mills
ill. by Dennis Nolan
Little, Brown & Co., 1995

Imagining/Writing

One afternoon when you are playing a game of pick-up sticks under a tree in your backyard, a little boy suddenly falls out of the tree and lands in the grass beside you. "Who are you?" you ask. "I'm a fairy," he says. But he doesn't have any wings.

At Home

Take home on a piece of cardboard and bake at 265°F (129°C) about 20 minutes (cardboard will not burn). Glue a pin backing down the center of the back with craft cement. Let dry for 24 hours.

19 **Elves:** Cut two tiny balls from purple scraps and press on the face for eyes. Cut a tiny ball of black from the remaining garlic-pressed strands, cut in half and press over the purple balls for irises. Make a toothpick hole for a mouth.
Fairies: Make the same kind of eyes from two tiny balls of blue scraps.

Gypsy Anklets

Supplies
- 3 hanks of #20 black hemp (120 feet or 36.6m)
- 2 hanks of thin black cord elastic (30 feet or 9.2m)
- 250 silver-colored beads (8 or 10mm)
- 160 silver dancing bells
- 10 pairs of scissors
- 5 rulers
- 5 bottles of white glue
- 10 paper punches
- 3 rolls of clear tape
- 6 small bowls
- cardboard

Each participant should have 12 feet (3.7m) of black hemp, 3 feet (91cm) of black cord elastic, 25 silver beads and 16 silver dancing bells.

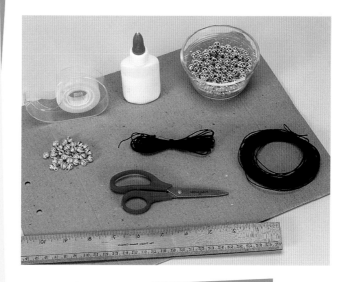

Preparation
Cut ten 10' (3m) lengths of hemp, ten 2' (60cm) lengths of hemp and ten 3' (91cm) lengths of elastic. Divide the silver beads and dancing bells into small bowls.

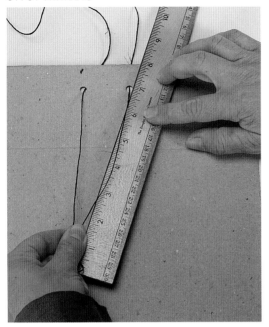

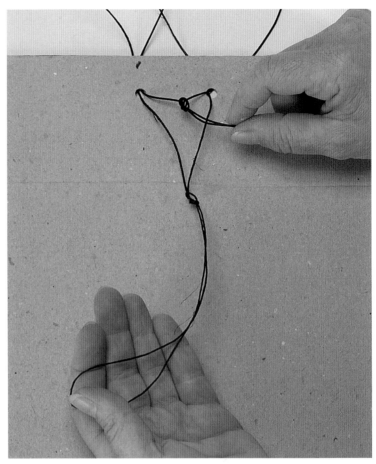

1 Fold the 10′ (3m) length of hemp in half. Tie off 6″ (15cm) with a loose overhand knot. Fold the elastic in half. Tie off 1″ (2.5cm) with a loose overhand knot. Punch two holes near top of a piece of cardboard 1½″ (4cm) apart. Thread an end of the hemp and elastic through each hole, centering the knots in the back.

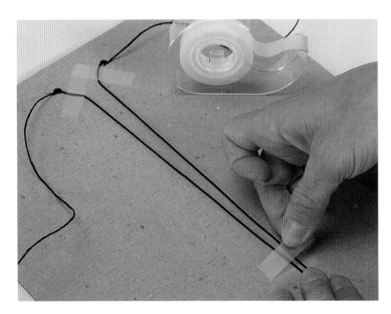

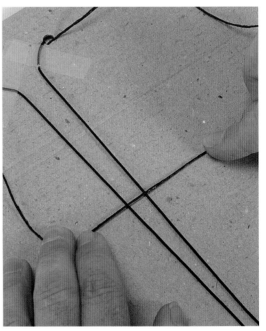

2 Tape the elastic on either side of the center front, bringing the ends together toward you down the center of the cardboard. Tape the ends together at the center bottom of the cardboard.

3 Tie six half-square knots: bring the left hemp string down about an inch (2.5cm), then right-angle it across the top of the elastic strings. Refer to the diagram on page 126.

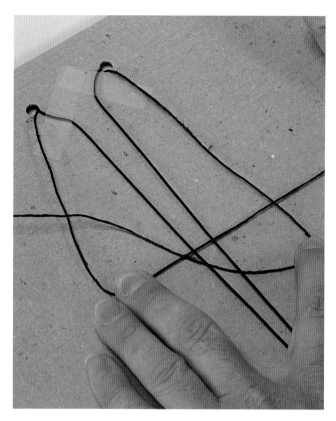

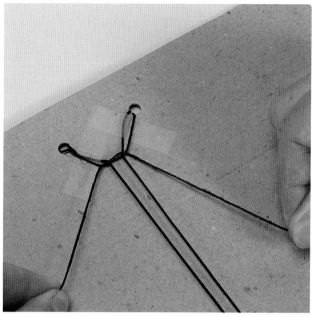

5 Pull snug, but not tight. Repeat five times.

4 Bring the right hemp string down over the end of the left string, and then pass it under all the strings on an upward diagonal.

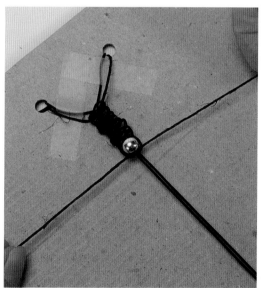

6 Untape the elastic and thread a silver bead up both strings. Retape.

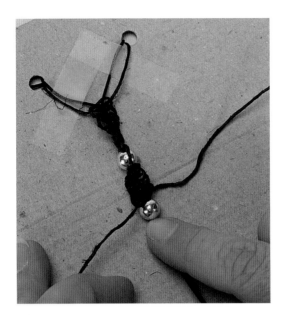

7 Bring the hemp threads around the bead and tie six more half-square knots.

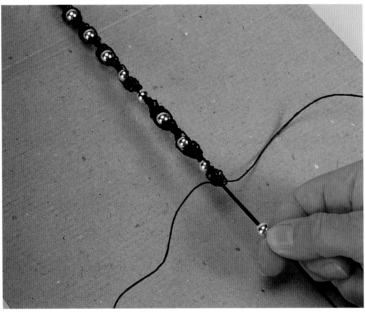

8 The knots will create a spiral pattern. Continue to add beads and tie six knots until the anklet measures about 1" (2.5cm) less than your ankle. End with a bead.

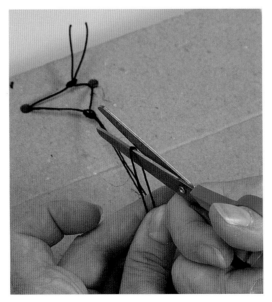

9 Cut the hemp and elastic loops and untie the anklet from the cardboard.

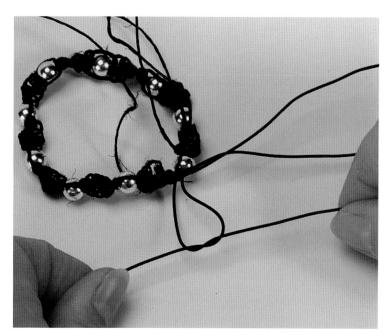

10 Tie the ends of the elastic on each edge of the anklet together with overhand knots. Tie the ends of the hemp on each edge of the anklet together with overhand knots, tying in the tied-off elastic just above the knot. Trim the elastic cords close to the knot and smooth the hemp ends to one side of the anklet.

11 Cut the 2′ (61cm) piece of hemp in half and thread it through each edge of the anklet on the opposite side from the tied-off ends. Find the middle of each piece and tie it together with an overhand knot.

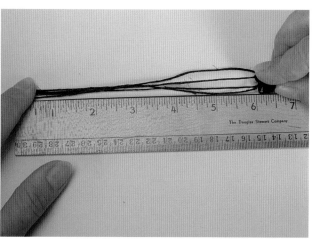

Featured Book
Gypsy Princess
by Phoebe Gilman
ill. by Phoebe Gilman
Scholastic, Inc. 1997

Cinnamon was happy being a wild gypsy girl. She lived in a gypsy caravan, read fortunes from her crystal ball, gathered herbs for her potions, spoke to the wind and danced with the bears. But her friend, Princess Cyprina, wants Cinnamon to live at the palace and become a princess. How can Cinnamon tell the kind princess how unhappy she is?

Related Books
A Small Miracle
by Peter Collington
ill. by Peter Collington
Random House, 1997

Savina, the Gypsy Dancer
by Ann Tompert
ill. by Denis Nolan
MacMillan, 1991

Imagining/Writing
Your Uncle Baal is getting married. He and his bride are going to need their own wagon to live in. Your father is going to build the wagon, and he's going to let you help.

12 Thread a silver bead on each of the strings. Tie an overhand knot under it, about 1" (2.5cm) from the anklet. Thread a second bead on each string. Tie an overhand knot under it, about 1" (2.5cm) from the first knot.

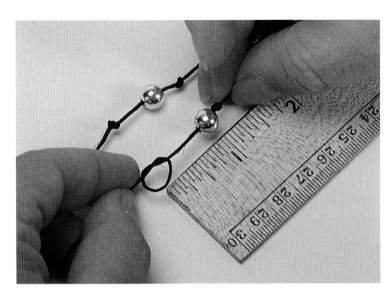

13 Thread two silver dancing bells on each string about 1" (2.5cm) from the second bead. Tie on with a double overhand knot. Trim the strings close to the knots.

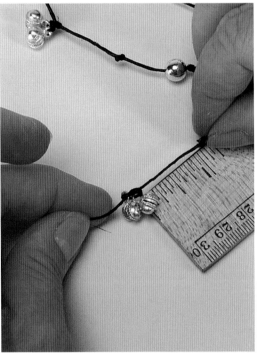

14 Put a drop of glue on each knot.

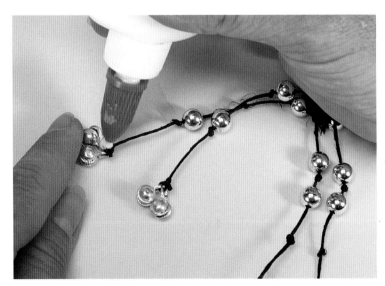

Sand and Sea Tops

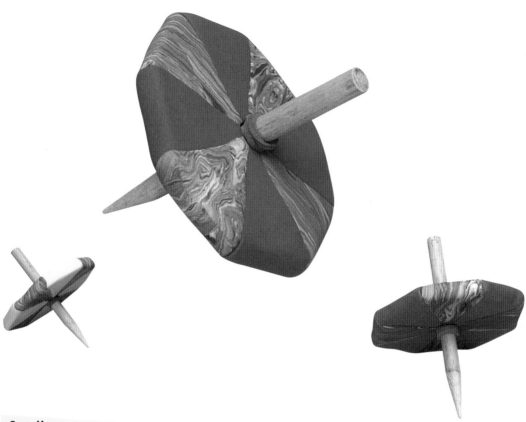

Supplies
- fifteen 2-oz. (56g) slabs of polymer clay: 5 white, 5 copper and 5 turquoise
- three 36" (91cm) long ¼" (6mm) wood dowels
- 10 plastic straws
- 60 colored rubber bands
- cardboard
- clay blades
- 5 rulers
- pencil sharpener
- mat knife

Each participant should have a half slab each of copper, turquoise and white clay, three 3" (8cm) pieces of sharpened wooden dowel, six colored rubber bands and one piece of cardboard.

Preparation
Cut the clay slabs in half. Trace the triangle pattern from page 125 onto cardboard and cut out ten. Trace the octagon pattern onto cardboard and cut three. Cut eighteen 6" (15cm) lengths from dowels. Sharpen each end of each piece to a point in the pencil sharpener. Cut each piece into two 3" (8cm) pieces.

1 Before starting, each participant should cut four more triangle patterns from cardboard. Cut the half-slabs of clay in half again, and then cut each quarter into four pieces.

2 Knead five pieces of the white clay into a ball. Roll into a sausage and flatten into a 1" × 2" (2.5cm × 2.5cm) rectangle about ½" (13mm) thick. Place four of the triangle patterns on top of the clay rectangle, lining up the short sides along both sides of the length.

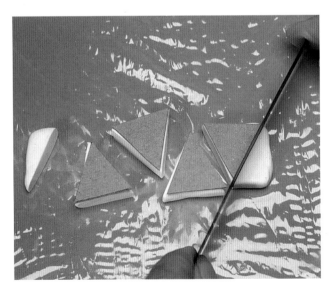

3 Cut between the patterns with a clay blade. Retain the four whole triangles; roll the half-triangles into a ball and return them to the pile of remaining pieces of white.

4 Repeat for the turquoise and then for the copper until you have four triangles of each color.

5 Roll the remaining pieces of each color into a ball. Roll each ball into a 2″ (5cm) sausage. Twist the sausages together and roll into a 8″ (20cm) sausage. Cut in four 2″ (5cm) lengths.

6 Twist and roll each length into a marbled ball.

7 Combine two marbled balls, roll into a sausage and flatten into a 1″ × 3″ (2.5cm × 8cm) rectangle. Repeat for the other two marbled balls. Place five triangle patterns on top of the clay rectangle, lining up the short sides along both sides of the length. Cut between the patterns with a clay blade.

8 Press your four remaining half-triangles together to make two complete triangles. Use the triangle pattern to retain the proper shape.

Featured Book
The Seashore Book
by Charlotte Zolotow
ill. by Wendell Minor
HarperCollins, 1994

"What is the seashore like?" the boy asks his mother. He lives in the mountains and has never seen the sea. With words of cold water and words of warm sand, feather and shell and wave words, mother paints a picture of the sea and the shore for him.

Related Books
The Big, Big Sea
by Martin Waddell
ill. by Jennifer Eachus
Candlewick Press, 1998

See the Ocean
by Estelle Condra
ill. by Linda Blassingame
Hambleton Hill Publishing, Inc., 1994

Imagining/Writing
I stood on the edge of the water and watched as a graceful seahorse swam in and out of the waves. I said to msyelf, "I wish I could trade places with that seahorse for just one hour!" And, suddenly my wish came true. I was the seahorse, and he was me.

9 Divide the pieces into three octagons, alternating patterned and solid colors. Press the triangles together; turn over and press together on the other side. Pat back into octagon shape using the octagon pattern.

10 Twist a hole in the center of each octagon with a plastic straw. Take home on a piece of cardboard and bake 265°F (129°C) for 20 minutes (cardboard will not burn). When cool, center each octagon on a piece of sharpened dowel.

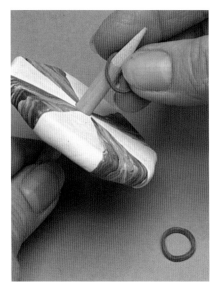

11 Secure with a rubber band on each side. Use a permanent black marker to decorate with letters or numbers if you wish to play traditional top games.

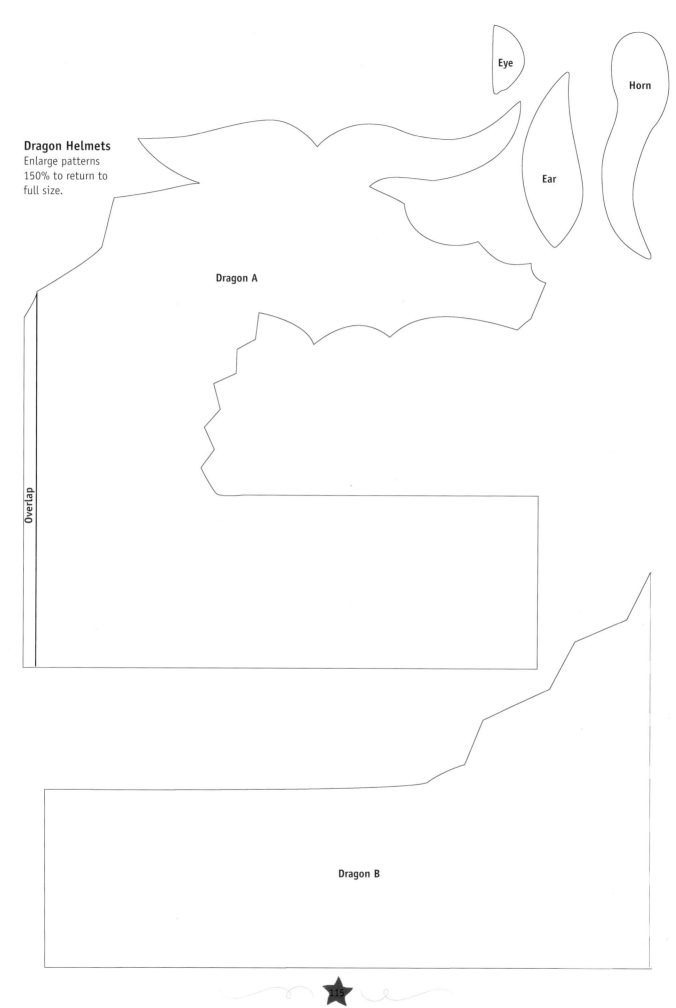

Dragon Helmets
Enlarge patterns
150% to return to
full size.

Eye

Horn

Ear

Dragon A

Overlap

Dragon B

Soft Felt Boxes
Enlarge patterns
200% to return to
full size.

Top

Bottom

Puffy Felt Stars

Enlarge patterns
125% to return to
full size.

Space Mobiles

Enlarge patterns
125% to return to
full size.

Small Star

Space Craft

Large Star

Moon, Sun, Earth

No-Sew Doll Pinafores

Enlarge patterns 200% to return to full size.

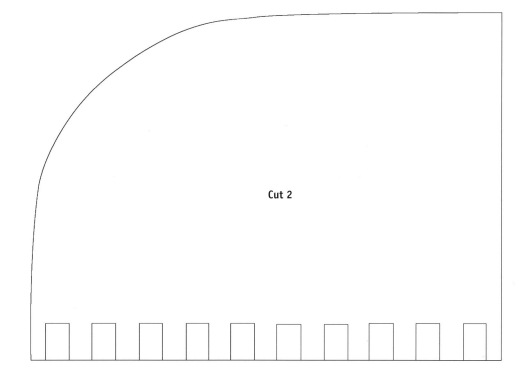

Cut 2

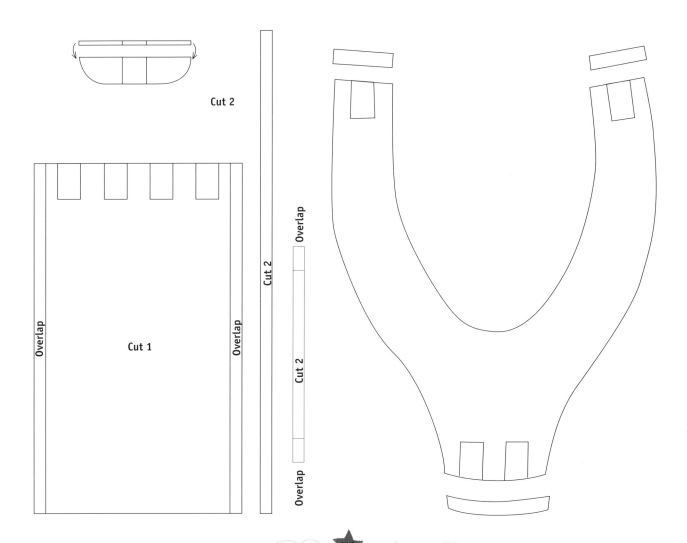

Cut 2

Cut 2

Cut 2

Cut 1

Overlap

Overlap

Overlap

Overlap

**Moon-and-Stars
Lantern**
Enlarge patterns
125% to return to
full size.

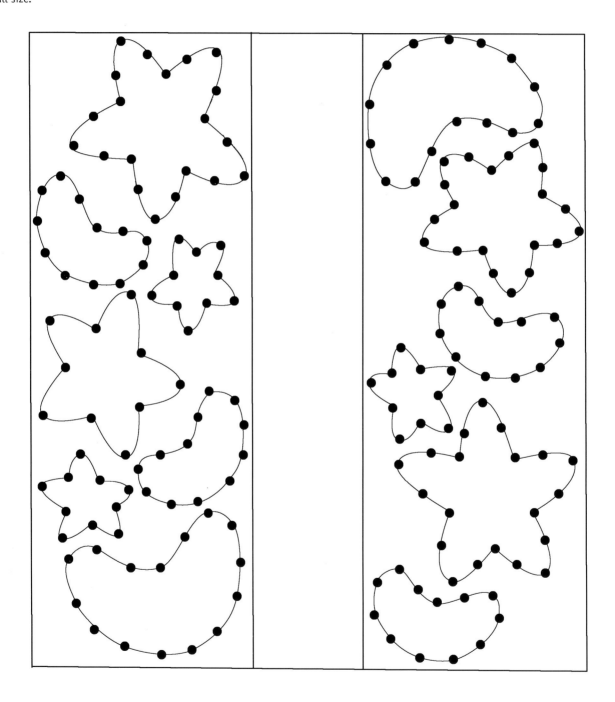

Frog Bookmarks
Pattern is full size.

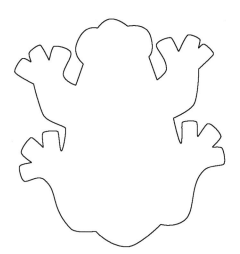

Folded Paper Birds
Pattern is full size.

Lizard Mola
Book Covers
Pattern is full size.

Refrigerator Pigs
Patterns are full size.

Collar

Hat

Flower

Fabric Maché Bowls
Patterns are full size.

Drowsy Mice
Patterns are full size

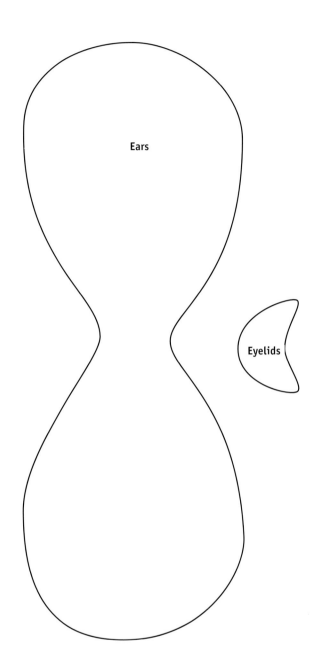

Ears

Eyelids

Flowerpot Pincushions
Pattern is full size

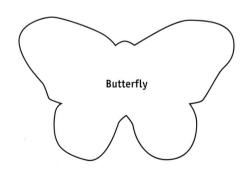

Butterfly

Bubble Wands
Pattern is full size

Elves and Fairies
Pattern is full size

Sand and Sea Tops
Patterns are full size

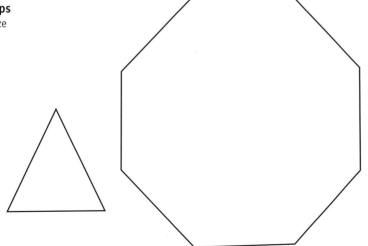

Macramé diagram

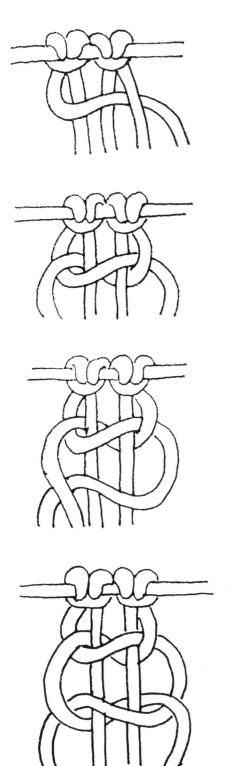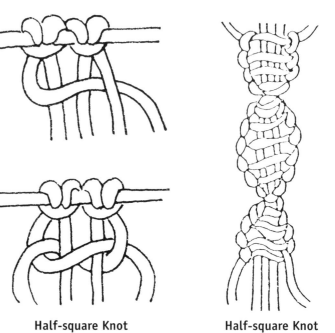

Half-square Knot

Half-square Knot

Square Knot

Index

Featured Children's Books

Amelia's Notebook
by Marissa Moss
ill. by Marissa Moss
Pleasant Co., 1999
Collage Scrapbooks

Apples and Pumpkins
by Anne Rockwell
ill. by Lizzy Rockwell
Simon & Schuster, 1989
Juggling Apples and Pumpkins

Big Al
by Andrew Clements
ill. by Yoshi
Simon & Schuster, 1997
Under-the-Sea Mobiles

The Biggest, Best Snowman
by Margery Cuyler
ill. by Will Hillenbrand
Scholastic Inc., 1998
Sock Snowmen

A Fairy Went A-Marketing
by Rose Fyleman
ill. by Jamichael Henterly
Penguin USA, 1991
Elves and Fairies

The Gardener
by Sarah Stewart
ill. by David Small
Farrar, Straus & Giroux, 2000
Flowerpot Pincushions

Gypsy Princess
by Phoebe Gilman
ill. by Phoebe Gilman
Scholastic Inc., 1997
Gypsy Anklets

The Hidden House
by Martin Waddell
ill. by Angela Barrett
Candlewick Press, 1997
No-Sew Doll Pinafores

How Many Bugs in a Box?
by David Carter
ill. by David Carter
Simon & Schuster, 1988
Soft Felt Boxes

The Iguana Brothers:
A Tale of Two Lizards
by Tony Johnston
ill. by Mark Teague
Scholastic Inc., 1995
Lizard Mola Book Covers

King Bidgood's in the Bathtub
(Caldecott Honor)
by Audrey Wood
ill. by Don Wood
Harcourt Brace & Co., 1993
Bubble Wands

Miss Spider's Tea Party
by David Kirk
ill. by David Kirk
Scholastic Inc., 1994
Magic Webs

Moon Festival
by Ching Yeung Russell
ill. by Christopher Zhong-Yuan
Zhang
Boyds Mill Press, 1997
Moon and Stars Lanterns

Nora's Stars
by Satomi Ichikawa
ill. by Satomi Ichikawa
Putnam Publishing, 1997
Puffy Felt Stars

The Paper Crane
by Molly Bang
ill. by Molly Bang
Morrow, William & Co., 1987
Folded Paper Birds

Piggie Pie!
by Margie Palantini
ill. by Howard Fine
Houghton Mifflin, 1997
Refrigerator Pigs

The Rag Coat
by Lauren Mills
ill. by Lauren Mills
Little, Brown & Co., 1991
Fabric Maché Bowls

Raising Dragons
by Jerdine Nolen
ill. by Elise Primavera
Harcourt Brace & Co., 1998
Dragon Helmets

Red-Eyed Tree Frog
by Joy Cowley
photos by Nic Bishop
Scholastic Inc., 1999
Frog Bookmarks

The Rough-Face Girl
by Rafe Martin
ill. by David Shannon
Putnam Publishing, 1998
Leather Bracelets

The Seashore Book
by Charlotte Zolotow
ill. by Wendell Minor
HarperCollins, 1994
Sand and Sea Tops

The Snow Speaks
by Nancy Carlstrom
ill. by Jane Dyer
Little, Brown & Co., 1995
Silver Snowflakes

Someplace Else
(Reading Rainbow)
by Carol Saul
ill. by Barry Root
Simon & Schuster, 1997
Love to Travel Pins

Space Case
by Edward Marshall
ill. by James Marshall
Penguin USA, 1982
Candy Corn Bracelets

The Worst Band in the Universe
by Graeme Base
ill. by Graeme Base
Harry N. Abrams, Inc., 1999
Space Mobiles

You Silly Goose
by Ellen Stoll Walsh
ill. by Ellen Stoll Walsh
Harcourt Brace & Co., 1996
Drowsy Mice

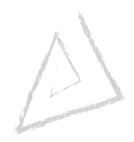